BLOOD FEUDS

Transcontinental Books
1100 René-Lévesque Boulevard West
24th floor
Montreal (Quebec) H3B 4X9
Tel.: 514 340-3587
Toll-free 1-866-800-2500
www.livres.transcontinental.ca

**Bibliothèque et Archives nationales du Québec and Library and
Archives Canada cataloguing in publication**

Main entry under title:
Blood feuds: hockey's best-ever rivalries
At head of title: The hockey news.

ISBN 978-0-9813938-1-0

1. Hockey - History - 20th century. 2. National Hockey League - History. 3. Violence in sports.
I. Kennedy, Ryan. II. Hockey news (Montréal, Québec).

GV846.5.B56 2010   796.962'6404   C2010-941199-4

Project editor: Ryan Kennedy
Art director: Annick Desormeaux
Cover design: Jamie Hogdson

Printed in Canada
© Transcontinental Books, 2010
Legal deposit — 3rd quarter 2010
National Library of Quebec
National Library of Canada

We acknowledge the financial support of the Government of Canada through the Canada
Book Fund for our publishing activities and the Government of Quebec through the SODEC
Tax Credit for our publishing activities.

For information on special rates for corporate libraries and wholesale purchases, please
call 1-866-800-2500.

The Hockey News

Edited by Ryan Kennedy

BLOOD FEUDS

HOCKEY'S BEST-EVER RIVALRIES

Transcontinental Books

Dedicated to Elizabeth S. Kennedy,
born and raised during the execution of this book.

Table of Contents

Introduction

The first thing anyone does in hockey is pick sides. Whether it's the team you support or whichever sibling is forced to don the goalie pads in the driveway, we distinguish ourselves by the flags we fly and the colors we wear.

And whether you believe sports mean everything in the world or nothing at all, there is no mistaking the passion that comes with following a game such as hockey. It becomes cultural, civic, even patriotic.

For the Czechoslovakians under Soviet rule in the 1960s and '70s, hockey was an outlet where the Big Red Machine could be held accountable and even defeated, if only on sheets of ice instead of the streets of Prague. In Saskatoon, defeating Regina meant a shot across the bow at the province's capital, ditto for Calgary's aggression towards Edmonton.

On a more visceral level, sometimes the blood spilled wasn't metaphorical; it was just blood. Hockey can be a swift and brutal game; it's the only mainstream team sport that still tolerates fisticuffs and allows players to settle injustices (and create a few new ones) right then and there on the ice.

For the uninitiated, it's a violent rite. But ask Colorado and Detroit fans; they'll tell you about the catharsis of seeing one's enemy struck down with a punch. Hockey is different and for many people, that frontier justice, that 'code,' is a great reason to follow the sport.

With *Blood Feuds*, we have taken the concept of the rivalry and applied it to every facet of the hockey world. From the NHL's past and present to the college, major junior and international ranks, it's not hard to find long-standing disagreements.

In the following pages you will find heroes and villains from all eras and all locales. Your job as a fan is to determine which ones are which. John Lennon and the Beatles weren't speaking on behalf of sports fans when they recorded their iconic anthem: Sometimes, all you need is hate.

VS. NEW YORK RANGERS
NEW YORK ISLANDERS

With apologies to the Buffalo Sabres, there's just one intra-New York State NHL rivalry worth talking about: the bright-lights, big-city glamour of the Original Six Rangers versus the sleepy-suburbia, commuter-community kitschiness of the expansion Islanders.

It began on June 6, 1972 when Long Island was awarded the state's third NHL franchise to begin play in the 1972-73 season. Brad Park was there from the beginning. He was already a Hall of Fame-caliber defenseman with the Rangers who would have won three Norris Trophies already if a certain guy named Bobby Orr wasn't in the midst of winning eight in a row. Park remembers those early days as anything but contentious; traveling to Nassau Veterans' Memorial Coliseum in Uniondale, N.Y., was a home-away-from-home game for the Rangers the first season or two.

> **"We would stay across the street, and the idea of going to the rink, just walking across the street, maybe 100 yards, I know I couldn't do it."**
> **– Denis Potvin**

"Basically they were a new team coming into Ranger territory, and trying to establish themselves," Park said. "The first couple years we went in there, it was like home games. They were all Rangers fans."

The Islanders won a grand total of 31 games in their first two seasons. But in their maiden playoff voyage in 1975 they made it to Round 3, toppling the Rangers in a best-of-three series along the way. And with that, the rancor that is the Empire State rivalry was born.

"We were kind of taking them seriously, but not really seriously," remembered Park of that '75 post-season. "They beat us in a two out of three, now you've got a piss-off contest."

A young, Hall-of-Fame-defenseman-to-be, Denis Potvin, was instrumental in that series win. He was the bounty of the Islanders' horrible, 12-win inaugural season. With the first overall pick in 1973, the Islanders nabbed the ready-for-prime-time blueliner.

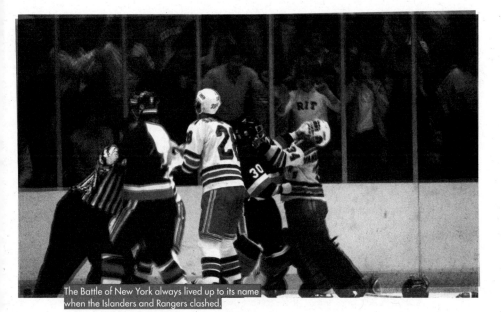

The Battle of New York always lived up to its name when the Islanders and Rangers clashed.

"That '75 playoff was a key moment in establishing the Islanders as a team, separating Long Island from New York City," Potvin said. "Now you definitely had two sides – people who would only root for the Islanders and Rangers fans. That series was the beginning of the rivalry."

And it was especially fierce for Potvin. Rangers star center Ulf Nilsson broke his ankle in 1979 after absorbing a particularly heavy hip check from Potvin. The Rangers faithful went nuts, and never forgave the blue-liner. A tradition was born and to this day cheers of 'Potvin sucks! Potvin sucks!' rain down from the stands at every Rangers home game punctuating the song *Let's Go Band*, regardless of the competition. And once the Rangers stopped playing the song to egg on the fans, the faithful just started humming or whistling it themselves so they could yell 'Potvin sucks!'

"Thirty-one years they've been doing that chant," said Potvin, a three-time Norris winner. "They do it now with a smile on their faces. When I did (color commentating) for the Panthers, people would turn around and say 'You suck Potvin.' "

There may be a good-natured vibe to the ribbing now, but it wasn't always so. New Yorkers are famous for how they treat opposing players, no matter the sport, and Potvin was one of their most reviled figures. Just getting from the hotel in Manhattan to the Garden was harrowing.

"Madison Square Garden could always be a dangerous place," Potvin recalled. "We would stay across the street, and the idea of going to the rink, just walking across the street, maybe 100 yards, I know I couldn't do it. I was so despised by Rangers fans, I couldn't walk those 100 yards.

"I left the hotel at 2:00 and 2:30 in the afternoon just to get to the rink. The idea of walking at 5:00 or 5:30 was out of the question, because all of those fans would be there and it was a real threat."

Potvin recalled one incident when the team bus was leaving the Garden and Rangers fans weren't going to let it go without a fight, despite the mounted police and riot unit on hand. As the bus slowly backed up through the mob, one fan threw a full beer at it. Islander Gord Lane was sitting next to a window, the bottle shattered it, leaving the defenseman with shards of glass in his face.

"That was the kind of treatment the Rangers fans (gave us)," Potvin said. "Those were the kinds of encounters we had."

For Potvin personally, the scariest incident took place during an MSG rendition of the national anthem. He was standing on the blueline with his helmet off, the lights were dimmed and a spotlight was on the anthem singer. Potvin felt something zip past his ear during the anthem, and when the lights came back up he saw that it was a nine-volt battery.

"Had that thing hit me from the upper deck or something, it would have been disastrous," Potvin said. "From that point on, they never turned the lights off, and they still don't."

Deadpanned Park when reminded of that story: "He's lucky they weren't throwing car batteries at him."

The Rangers-Islanders rivalry was most heated during the late 1970s. The Islanders were a team on the rise, having drafted a nucleus – Potvin, Bob Nystrom, Clark Gillies, Bryan Trottier, Mike Bossy – that led them to four consecutive Stanley Cups to kick off the 1980s. The Rangers were an up-and-down squad – good one year, not so much the next – but might have ended a 39-year Cup drought in 1979 if not for Potvin's hit on Nilsson.

"The '78 and '79 seasons were so emotional," Potvin said. "(The rivalry) really reached its peak around that point."

It may have peaked in the '70s, but it didn't die; it's just been muted by some middling-to-poor results in recent seasons.

The Rangers have just one Cup in the past 70 years and went through a stretch where they missed the playoffs seven straight years during the 1990s and 2000s. The Islanders have been even worse, missing the post-season 13 of the past 20 seasons and not getting past the first round since 1993.

But the rivalry can flare up again at any time. All it takes is an accelerant. "I remember sitting in the dressing room and I could just hear the crowd going nuts," said goaltender Glenn Healy of his first taste of the rivalry during the 1989-90 season while with the Islanders. "I'm thinking 'What is that noise?' and one of the guys said 'That's the crowd. This is an Islanders-Rangers game. This thing's enormous.'

"And that was, like, two hours before the game. They were already in their seats, wild."

As so many do, the Rangers-Islanders rivalry gets especially heated when the two sides meet in the playoffs. That last happened in 1990. And as has so often been the case, the Madison Square Garden fans were front and center.

Islanders star Pat Lafontaine was seriously injured in Game 2 of the teams' first round series, sending the Rangers faithful into a frenzy of series-winning anticipation.

"They wouldn't let the ambulance leave the building," said Healy, who later saw things from the other side as a Ranger. "They were rocking the ambulance. That's about as intense as you're going to get."

One theory for just why the Islanders are so hated by Rangers fans is that the Islanders are kind of like the little brother who took all the abuse, but then grew up and kicked his brother's ass.

"It's a huge rivalry in the sense that the Rangers are New York's team, but yet, it's the Islanders that are the dynasty; they're the ones who have won the championships," Healy said.

And once that winning started, all of those Rangers fans who couldn't get tickets in Manhattan and went out to the Isle instead, found themselves either unable to get their hands on any ducats or severely outnumbered if they did.

Healy's favorite Islanders fans during his stint with the team from 1989 to 1993 were two who used to wear their jerseys in the Ranger blue section of Nassau Coliseum. One had No. 19 on his back, the other No. 40. When standing next to each other, they were a very visible reminder of the Rangers' last Cup victory, 50-some-odd years before in 1940.

"You've never seen two guys get chased out of a building faster," Healy laughed.

Veteran sportswriter – and former Rangers employee Stan Fischler – recalls that sort of slight going back even further. "First of all, the most important thing to remember is that there was a constant theme that was rubbed in over and over again by Islander fans, and that was the chant '1940! 1940!' " Fischler noted. "Whenever the Rangers played out in Long Island, they'd be ripped: '1940! 1940!' "

The rivalry is waiting for its next accelerant, whether that's a playoff series featuring the two teams as in 1990, a battle for the Atlantic Division crown, or a Cup win for either franchise. But regardless, it's still there, simmering. And to a certain extent it still means a lot, especially to the long-suffering Islanders fans, who've had little to cheer about other than the draft lottery recently.

"That's the Islanders' Stanley Cup right now," Healy said of the season series with the Rangers. "Those games mean a lot more than just your regular games. A lot more."

VS. CAM NEELY
ULF SAMUELSSON

It was so intense, it really could be scary.

"Incredible," said Mark Recchi, a witness to several epic battles between his Pittsburgh Penguins teammate, defenseman Ulf Samuelsson, and Cam Neely, the Boston Bruins' Hall of Fame-bound right winger. "I was glad I was watching it, and not part of it."

The rivalry between the 6-foot-1, 218-pound Neely and Samuelsson, who was listed at 6-1, 205, peaked during the 1991 Eastern Conference final, when Neely sustained injuries that eventually led to premature retirement. Post-season intensity wasn't the only reason such all-out war was waged, though.

Neely and Samuelsson were in each other's faces and at each other's throats from the moment Neely became a Bruin, via trade with

Ulf Samuelsson's job was always to slow down Cam Neely.

Vancouver, prior to the 1986-87 season. Samuelsson, a draftee from Sweden, arrived in Hartford in 1984-85 and was blossoming into a physical (162 penalty minutes), competent (plus-28) shutdown defense-man when Neely came to the Adams Division for eight annual vicious regular-season meetings between the New England neighbors.

Neely, relatively anonymous over his first three seasons with the Canucks (he averaged 17 goals), quickly became synonymous with the term "power forward." He had great hands around the net and his shot was feared, but he also left teams wary of his tremendous hits on the fore-check, as well as his ability – and even eagerness – to fight.

Just as quickly, Samuelsson was the defenseman assigned by the Whalers to try to keep Neely contained. Like few others, Samuelsson wasn't afraid to check (face-to-face or from behind), cross-check, elbow, knee or punch Neely during ferocious shifts in Hartford territory. Neely, by now a developing star and fan favorite in Boston and across the NHL, gave back whatever he hadn't dished out, and vice versa.

"I totally understood where Samuelsson was coming from, and what his job was," said Andy Brickley, who joined Neely and the B's in 1988-89. "It was to preoccupy Cam, get him off his game, whatever it took, and no matter how badly his image was marred as a result. He didn't care. He really didn't."

As enraged as Neely could become because Samuelsson wouldn't fight, he was generally successful against the Whalers in the early years of the rivalry. Most notably, he helped the Bruins survive the temporary absence of Hall of Fame defenseman Ray Bourque in a first-round play-off in 1990, putting up 4-6-10 scoring totals over seven games, including a game-winning goal in Game 5. He piled up 27 penalty minutes in that series; Samuelsson collected 18.

"I just didn't respect the way the guy played."
- Cam Neely

"It was a monumental effort for Cam to not get pre-occupied with (Samuelsson)," Brickley said. "With that game within a game, those 1-on-1 confrontations, it was so hard for him to just stay the course and play his game. He had plenty of nights when he did, but some nights when he just couldn't."

Samuelsson's trade to Pittsburgh at the 1991 deadline only served to accelerate the battle. The already powerful Penguins, further fortified by ex-Whalers Samuelsson and center Ron Francis, met the favored Bruins in the conference final, with the Neely-Samuelsson match-up attracting almost as much pre-series attention as that given to names like Bourque, Mario Lemieux, Paul Coffey and Jaromir Jagr. Neely scored the Game 1 winner and helped the Bruins take a 2-0 lead in the series, but Pittsburgh charged back to win in six games en route to the first of consecutive Stanley Cups.

One of the indelible images of the series is a knee-on-knee hit with which Samuelsson upended Neely in open ice.

"Every series there is something that draws attention, makes it emotional, and that was in that series, I guess," Samuelsson said. "I was trying to hit his shoulder, but I guess he moved at the last second, and I hit his knee...I wasn't trying to take him out."

Neely, however, had actually sustained more significant damage earlier in the series. While trying to hit Samuelsson in a corner, he sustained a thigh injury that led to a condition known as myositis ossificans, where damaged muscle begins to turn to bone.

"They played on the edge, both of them," Recchi said. "They were both going to do whatever it took to win a hockey game. On one shift, Cam would get the better of Ulf, and the next Ulf would get the better of Cam. Neither one of them was going to back down.

"They'd drawn a line in the sand, and they were going to go. That's why both teams were where they were at. We were both in the (Stanley Cup) semis because guys like that were willing to take it to the edge, and do whatever it took to win."

Confrontations between Neely and Samuelsson were rare after '91. Thigh and knee injuries limited Neely to just 26 games over the 1991-92 and '92-93 seasons, and led to hip damage that forced him to retire after the 1996-97 season.

Neely and Samuelsson never had a bygones-be-bygones discussion. ("We haven't talked at all," Samuelsson said.) Neely no longer discusses the matter, simply saying "my feelings haven't changed."

In one of the last interviews in which he addressed the rivalry, the impression is left that had Samuelsson been more willing to settle matters with his fists (they only fought twice, in 1990 and '93, with Neely getting instigator penalties both times), things may not have ended quite so bitterly.

"I just didn't respect the way the guy played," Neely said. "If you play a certain way...you know you're going to upset some people, and you've got to be prepared to drop your gloves and go at it and settle your differences."

As things played out, each Neely vs. Samuelsson meeting was the 1-on-1 equivalent of one of the NHL's oldest, most storied rivalries: Montreal vs. Boston.

"To see that kind of hatred, that was really relegated for us toward the Canadiens, focused on one guy – it was so similar," Brickley said. "That's one of the things that makes it so memorable."

VS. CAL GARDNER
KEN REARDON

Cal Gardner had a vicious running feud with Montreal's Ken Reardon.

One of hockey's most legendary feuds resulted from what was perhaps an accidental collision.

The Montreal Canadiens were playing the New York Rangers on March 16, 1947. With Montreal leading 4-3 in the late stages of the contest, Canadiens defenseman Ken Reardon carried the puck up ice.

Rangers forward Bryan Hextall nailed Reardon with a bodycheck, knocking him off balance and sending him crashing face-first into the stick of Rangers forward Cal Gardner.

The blow from Gardner's stick cut Reardon for 14 stitches and dislodged several teeth.

"My upper lip felt as if it had been sawed off my face," Reardon told writer Stan Fischler in a 1962 *Sports Illustrated* interview.

Whether the blow was intentional is a matter that has been debated for years.

"He was mean and he certainly knew how to use his stick," said Howie Meeker of Gardner, later a teammate of his in Toronto.

In Reardon's mind, there was no doubt – Gardner had done it intentionally. Two years later, on New Year's Day 1949 at Maple Leaf Gardens, after Gardner had been dealt to Toronto, Reardon sought to exact his revenge.

The two rivals engaged in a vicious stick-swinging duel during the second period of play. Gardner broke his stick across Reardon's shoulder, and then the two dropped the gloves. NHL president Clarence Campbell fined Gardner $250 and Reardon $200, suspending both from the next Montreal-Toronto game.

> **"I asked Reardon, 'Mr. Reardon, is it true that you said on the ice that you wanted to jam your stick down Mr. Gardner's throat?' "**
> **- Clarence Campbell**

"The Reardon-Gardner case is now closed," read a statement issued by Campbell. But like the Hatfields and the McCoys, the feud continued. During a Nov. 10, 1949 game at the Montreal Forum, Reardon shattered Gardner's jaw with an elbow.

End of the feud? Hardly. In the March 1950 issue of *Sport* magazine, Reardon made it clear that vengeance remained on his mind.

"I'm going to see that Gardner gets 14 stitches in the mouth," Reardon said. "I may have to wait a long time, but I'm patient. Even if I have to wait until the last game I ever play, Gardner is going to get it good and plenty."

This drew the ire of Campbell, who called both men on the carpet.

"I asked Reardon, 'Mr. Reardon, is it true that you said on the ice that you wanted to jam your stick down Mr. Gardner's throat?' " Campbell recounted in a 1982 interview with James Christie of the *Globe & Mail*. " 'Yes,' he said. 'And the next time we're out there, I'll make sure I do it.' "

Campbell moved to put a stop to the rivalry. "Having prior knowledge of what he was going to do, I couldn't just let it go at that," he said.

Reardon was forced to post a $1,000 good conduct bond, money he'd forfeit if he went after Gardner. The money was refunded to Reardon when he retired following the 1949-50 season, but the bitterness lingered.

Both men were appropriately featured in *Forever Rivals*, a 1996 documentary about the Leafs and Canadiens.

"I wouldn't lower myself to talk to him," said Gardner, who died in 2001, during the show.

Countered Reardon, who died in 2008, "If I played one more year, I would have had one more go, because a $1,000 fine is not that much money."

VS. DON CHERRY
EUROPEANS

Don Cherry can get pretty worked up when talking about European hockey players; especially the ones he likes.

"My favorite Russian, except when he slew-footed a guy and I called him a weasel, was Pavel Bure," Cherry said. "I always thought he was absolutely terrific."

OK, so even when Cherry praises Euros, there tends to be a qualifier. But even if Bure wasn't above some bashing from Canada's notoriously outspoken homer, it didn't seem to bother the slick Russian.
"He'd come right in the studio sometimes to say hello," Cherry said. "I really liked Pavel Bure, he was my type of player; gutsy little guy."

It's fair to say those words represent the exception to the rule regarding Cherry's feelings toward European players. Maybe it started when Cherry, in his one-year stint as Colorado Rockies coach back in 1979-80, was wedded to Hardy Astrom in goal, a man Cherry has previously referred to as the 'Swedish Sieve.'

Don Cherry has always been a fervent supporter of Canadian hockey talent.

Truth be told, even if Astrom had been Dominik Hasek, it's hard to imagine Cherry's views on players from across the pond changing too much. There's a bred-in-the-bone element to his hockey views and he's been only too happy to share them throughout 30 years as Canada's most prominent hockey commentator.

It's not that Cherry doesn't believe there's a place for Euros in the game; he just feels they have to bring something unique to the table.

"If the Russian is better and can score better and do everything better, that's fine," he said. "But don't give me guys who can score 12 or 13 goals. Canadians can do that."

Even the staunchest pro-Canadian supporter will concede European players have toughened up over the years. The question is are they thin-skinned when it comes to Cherry's comments, or does his take on them just gently roll off their backs like a soft pass from Nicklas Lidstrom's stick?

Bruce Dowbiggin is a *Globe and Mail* columnist who's had his run-ins with Cherry over the course of his long career in newspapers, TV and radio. He tends to believe Euros haven't been crazy about some of the opinions offered by the High-Collared One. Dowbiggin also thinks the fact people started tuning in en masse to hear Cherry's black-and-white stance only spurred a former coach looking to cement himself in a new career to keep pushing the envelope.

"I definitely think the Europeans are hurt by comments like that," Dowbiggin said. "That's not something anyone likes to hear.

"I still think it's an act." - Bruce Dowbiggin

"But for Don, I think it's all an act. When it first happened, the response was such that it made him more popular and because of that he played it up. That's not to say Don wasn't burned by any Europeans (when he coached in the NHL) and so to some degree he might believe (his anti-European stance), but when he's given a promotion or raise every time he calls someone a 'chicken Swede,' why wouldn't he continue to do it? I know he got mad at me once when I told him I thought it was all an act, but I still think it's an act."

For his part, Cherry steadfastly claims the views people hear from him are simply what's in his heart.

"That's the way I feel," he said. "I'd like to say, 'No, I don't feel that way,' but I believe in Canadian hockey players because I'm Canadian."

His interaction with Bure aside, Cherry said he rarely crosses paths with players, so the occasion for a European to exchange opinions doesn't frequently come up.

"They don't talk to me," he said. "I don't talk to many guys."

Scott Moore has been the executive director of CBC Sports since 2007, giving him a fairly intimate view into what the world of Cherry is all about. In his mind, Cherry's opinions are authentic, though they may be a little more malleable than people initially give him credit for.

"He has softened his view over time," Moore said. "You do hear him pay compliments to European players from time to time. He's not as dismissive (of them) as a group as he used to be."

If Cherry has undergone a metamorphosis, it certainly hasn't been at the behest of his CBC superiors. When Cherry first came onto the TV scene in the early 1980s, longtime *Hockey Night* executive director

Ralph Mellanby fought hard to keep him on air when many thought Cherry's rudimentary grasp of the English language made him better suited for another line of work.

Three decades later, Moore says he and Cherry speak often, but he's not about to ask a man who has entrenched himself in Canadian culture to start altering his stripes now.

"I don't want to change Don too much, especially in the latter years of his career," Moore said.

At this point, there's no denying Cherry is what he is. But Dowbiggin believes there is a divide with regard to how Cherry's years of rants and outrageous suits are perceived.

"I think for the younger population he's viewed as a kind of Mr. Burns, a cartoon character of sorts, a guy with a lot of bluster, but not much substance," Dowbiggin said. "For the older viewers, I think there's a real like for Don; he's a guy who was frank and backed up what he said.

"He came on the (*Hockey Night*) scene after Howie Meeker, who was all fussy and detail-oriented. Here was Don with his insights and edge and he was refreshing, and it was like listening to (comedians) Steven Wright or Henny Youngman, and he was popular. But since then he's become a self-parody of himself and I don't know if his views are endorsed by a lot of people anymore."

Whatever their take, people still tune in and that's the bottom line for Moore when it comes to Canada's most recognizable hockey-talker.

'There are many things about Don that make me chuckle or have a reaction, but the reality with Don is that he's a superstar in this country," Moore said. "One of the reasons – if not *the* reason – is people have a reaction to him, both positive and negative. The positive way outweighs the negative."

> **"Don't give me guys who can score 12 or 13 goals. Canadians can do that."**
> **– Don Cherry**

VS. FINLAND
SWEDEN

Even though two out of the three European players who've scored more than 600 NHL goals are Finns – Teemu Selanne and Jari Kurri – Finland is still not known for skilled snipers or silky-handed playmakers. Finland is famous for its goaltenders, which is perfectly in line with the national temperament. Finns are self-proclaimed loners – hard-working, yes, but loners. The strong, silent type.

Two major Finnish literary classics – *The Unknown Soldier* and *Under the North Star*, both by Vaino Linna – depict heroes that go at it alone. In *The Unknown Soldier* it's Rokka, an aloof sniper, while *Under the North Star* begins with "In the beginning, there were the marsh, the hoe – and Jussi." Jussi is a pioneer, clearing marshland to create a croft to live in.

Maybe it's not surprising then that Vaino Linna's son, Petteri, was a Finnish SM-liiga goalie in the late 1980s.

Being alone between the pipes – the last man standing – is perfect for Finns who are, geographically, stuck between one of the biggest countries in the world, Russia, and the one that thinks it's the biggest in the world, Sweden.

It may be genetic. According to the Finnish Institute for Molecular Medicine, "Finns are unique on the genetic map of Europe; (they) differ considerably both from Central Europeans and from (their) neighbors to the east. Genetically, Finns have more in common with, for example, the Dutch or Russians living in the area of Murom to the east of Moscow, than with our linguistic relations, the Hungarians."

Note: Not a mention of the neighbors to the west.

"They're like big brothers, and you want to beat your big brothers."
- Teemu Selanne on playing Sweden

Swedes are different. They've had ABBA, Mats Sundin, Ingmar Bergman, Peter Forsberg, Volvo, Saab, Anders Hedberg, Ingrid Bergman, Greta Garbo, Mats Naslund, Markus Naslund, Drago (Rocky's opponent in *Rocky IV*, played by Dolph Lundgren), Hakan Loob and IKEA. While a Finnish man will spend an entire day swearing as he tries to put together

The Finns are always trying to even the score with the Swedes.

IKEA's Billy bookshelf, the Swedes turn it into a family event where everybody can be involved, trying to figure out how the shelf is put together – and maybe that was the whole purpose, anyway.

Until 1809, Finland and Sweden were a single country; there's a sizable Swedish-speaking minority in Finland and Finns are the largest minority group in Sweden, thanks to immigration in the lean post-war years in Finland.

Finland and Sweden are like Newman and Seinfeld – "Newman!" – and the rest of the world is like George Costanza – "You think you're better than me?" – or Donald Duck and his cousin Gladstone Gander, a lazy and infuriatingly lucky fowl who never fails to upset Donald. That is the most fitting comparison, considering the fact that the Donald Duck comic is the biggest weekly publication in Finland and that Finns them-selves relate strongly to Donald.

Sweden's the big brother; the lucky goose.

"Individually, I don't know one bad Swedish guy, but as a team, you always want to beat them," Selanne said. "They're like big brothers, and you want to beat your big brothers."

Hockey, being the biggest sport in both countries – and one where both Sweden and Finland are world class – becomes the vessel for all those emotions.

Finland played its first-ever game against Sweden, and lost 8-1 in 1928.

> **"Personally, I love to see Sweden beat Canada. It's just tougher." - Mattias Ek**

Sweden won the World Championship in 1953, 1957, 1962 and 1987 before Finland had even won a medal. A silver at the Calgary Olympics helped the Finns (Sweden finished with a bronze), but the Swedes managed to get another World Championship gold in 1991, a year before the Finns earned their first medal at the worlds (a silver).

At the 1986 worlds, Finland had a 4-2 lead against Sweden with 40 seconds remaining, but somehow Anders 'Masken' Carlsson netted two and tied the game, giving Sweden the point it needed to get to the medal round, where it finished second. Finland finished fourth.

In 1991, Finland had a 4-2 lead with 52 seconds remaining, when Mats Sundin got Sweden to within a goal and, 15 seconds later, tied the game. Sweden went on to win the World Championship. Finland wound up fifth.

Between 1970 and 1979, Sweden's Tre Kronor won nine World Championship medals, three silvers and six bronzes. Finland's record in the same period: 4th, 4th, 4th, 4th, 4th, 4th, 5th, 5th, 7th and 5th.

In 1987, Finland lost a game against (West) Germany, but after it became clear the Germans had used a non-eligible, Polish-born player who'd previously represented Poland in an IIHF tournament, the score was overturned and Finland awarded the win. The Swedes brought the case to a civil court in Vienna and won; the IIHF had to reverse the ruling, again making Finland the loser. Finland wound up in the relegation round, while Sweden played for a medal. The Swedes ended up winning the tournament.

At the 2003 World Championship in Helsinki, Finland, the home side had a 5-1 lead against Sweden in the quarterfinal halfway through the game. To make a long story short, the Swedes – with Sundin – won the game 6-5.

Of course, there are also the times when Finland has done well, just not as well as Sweden. In 1992, Finland won its first-ever World Championship medal, a silver. The Finns lost just one game in the tournament: 5-2 against the Swedes, in the final. At the 2006 Turin Olympics, Finland also lost just one game: the final against Sweden, 4-3.

It's easy to see why the Finns have adopted the role of unlucky Donald Duck. What makes matter worse is the fact that Swedes don't seem to care about beating the Finns as much.

"Swedes like to beat Finland because we know that they get a kick out of beating us in a major tournament," said Mattias Ek, a reporter at Swedish *Expressen*, who has covered many a 'Finnkampen' – 'Finn fight' – as the term is known in Swedish. "Personally, I love to see Sweden beat Canada. It's just tougher."

After a recent European soccer championship draw that saw Finland and Sweden end up in the same pool, the Finnish papers ran headlines that read "It's us against Sweden." Swedish papers proclaimed "We'll play Holland."

Finns don't care if they lose, as long as the Swedes don't win. But the Swedish media always gets behind Finland if Tre Kronor is out of the competition – like in the Vancouver Olympics.

Of course Finland's won some, too. In 1998 at the Nagano Games, Finland beat Sweden in the quarterfinal. And in 1995, the Finns beat Sweden in the World Championship final in Stockholm. Finland went crazy. Fighter planes escorted the team home and more than 100,000 people gathered in downtown Helsinki for a parade.

For a generation of Finns, that was a dream come true. But it's been 15 years now and a new generation is starting to dream the same dream. A nightmare.

VS. UNIVERSITY OF WISCONSIN
UNIVERSITY OF MINNESOTA

Minnesota and Wisconsin share a long border and a long tradition of collegiate hockey, but not much else.

On one side is American's Dairyland with its farms, fields and contented cows. Wisconsin is peopled with 'cheeseheads' known for their proliferate dairy production and profligate drinking culture.

On the other side is the North Star State, the Land of 10,000 Lakes. Minnesota is a little more urban with its Twin Cities and urbane citizens known for impeccable manners and politeness – their 'Minnesota nice.'

"There's the feeling (in Minnesota) that, 'Hey, we're a little more urban, a little more upscale and you guys are still farmers'," said Rob Andringa, Wisconsin's TV broadcaster and a former Badgers player (1987-1991). "In the back of their minds they view it as, 'We're still a superior hockey force. It's like Canada. Every kid grows up playing hockey.'

"If they want to believe that, I'm all for it and I'll find ways to argue it."

Wisconsin does have six NCAA national championships to Minnesota's five, though it's hard to argue against Minnesota's overall domination of Wisconsin with its 152-83-18 lifetime record. But the Badgers do hold the trump card – the single sweetest victory ever between the two rivals: a 6-3 win in Minnesota for the 1981 NCAA title, the only time they've met in the Frozen Four final.

"There's a natural irritation between Minnesota and Wisconsin." – Doug Woog

The teams have a storied rivalry. But whenever they meet, far more than collegiate credentials is at stake. State pride is on the line.

"When (the Badgers) played the Gophers, they knew they weren't just playing against the University of Minnesota," said Todd Richards, Minnesota Wild coach and a former Gophers player (1985-89). "They were playing against the State of Minnesota."
It's the same for Wisconsin.

Sharing a border hasn't made Minnesota and Wisconsin anywhere near neighborly when it comes to college hockey.

The rivalry began in the 1960s when Wisconsin re-started its program after a 28-year absence. Making the Gophers their main rival was easy.

"There's a natural irritation between Minnesota and Wisconsin," said Doug Woog, Minnesota's TV broadcaster and a former Gophers player (1965-66) and coach (1985-99). "And it isn't relegated only to hockey."

Back in the bad old days, the Badgers couldn't match the skill of the seasoned Gophers system, going strong since the 1920s. Wisconsin had a few football players on the team, so their strategy often had a slightly gridiron flavor.

"We caught them in the breaking-in period when their guys would play like football players," Woog said. "The linebackers would take a run at you and then another linebacker or defensive end would come at you the other way. Seldom did they make contact, but they made a lot of noise and created a lot of fear.

"Minnesota thought they played a cleaner more collegiate style of hockey whereas they thought the Badgers were more willing to fight than to score."

The hate-meter hit its high during the 70s under Hall of Fame coaches Herb Brooks and Bob Johnson. Brooks brought NCAA titles to Minnesota in '74, '76 and '79 for the Gophers, while Johnson won in '73 and '77 for the Badgers (Johnson was behind the bench in '81, but Brooks wasn't). The two coaches mirrored the same animosity and bad blood between their teams.

"(It was) sheer hatred for each other," said Andringa, Johnson's neighbor growing up and whose father was the team doctor for Johnson's '76 U.S. Olympic team. "Bob and Herb were the most competitive guys you'll ever hear about.

"They didn't like each other because they were so successful and yet they were completely different on how they went about coaching the game and recruiting. Herbie was an intense fiery coach. Bob, on the other hand, was a little more free-flowing, always coming up with the positive."

The competitive juices weren't limited to players and coaches, though. Fans and bands often employed some interesting tactics, especially Wisconsin's. The Badgers' boisterous student section includes its band, which used to hang its horns over the glass in the early days when it was shorter and blast away in the visitors' end while the team warmed up. Gopher players would respond by picking them off one by one with their sticks.

The mercury has dropped slightly in recent years, but there's no chance the hate will ever dissipate. Their love of hockey notwithstanding, the differences between the two states will always give Minnesota and Wisconsin reasons to not like each other.

"That just keeps the blood boiling, which I like," Andringa said. "I know this; I definitely disliked the Gophers when I played them."

"Sheer hatred."
- Rob Andringa

REGINA PATS
SASKATOON BLADES

Saskatchewan's two biggest cities are represented by the Pats and Blades.

Memories? Oh, sure. Stu Grimson has plenty.

Talking over the phone from his office in Nashville, the hockey enforcer-turned-lawyer takes a few seconds to reflect on a part of his past that is 25 years old. Where to begin? There were the fights, of course. Line brawls, bench-clearing brawls, brawling in the stands and brawling in the parking lot.

You name it, Grimson saw it. Or, in most cases, the player known as the 'Grim Reaper' started it.

But the ongoing feud between the Western League's Regina Pats and Saskatoon Blades was not just about players and fans punching each other silly. No, this rivalry was about more than hockey. It was part provincial. It was part little brother trying to step out from big brother's shadow. Most importantly, it was about winning some civic pride.

"I probably didn't appreciate it to the full extent," says Grimson, who played for the Pats from 1982-83 to 1984-85. "But I remember being in high school and in the days leading up to the game there was this energy throughout the city. Everyone cared that we won. It didn't matter if it was an exhibition game or whatever. That was the one game where we couldn't lose.

"You knew that this wasn't any other team that we were playing. You knew you had to have your helmet buckled."

Talk to anyone who has played for the Pats or Blades – or had tickets to any of their head-to-head games – and it seems like it has always been this way. Sure, the Saskatoon Blades also really dislike the Prince Albert Raiders and the Regina Pats have their hate-on for the Moose Jaw Warriors. But when the Blades meet the Pats, something different is in the air.

> **"I still hear cat-calls all the time, whether I'm in the arenas or walking on the streets."**
> **- Lorne Molleken**

"I think it goes back to the Louis Riel days," joked former Blades GM and coach Daryl Lubiniecki. "There always was and there always will be a rivalry. It doesn't matter who's playing for what team. It wouldn't even matter if it was curling. If the Pats and Blades were playing, there would have been a brawl."

Familiarity is what breeds most rivalries. The more two teams play each other, the more history they have. Saskatoon and Regina go back to their days in the Saskatchewan Junior League. But the root of their rivalry can be located on a football field, not a hockey rink.

Saskatoon is the largest city in Saskatchewan. But Regina (the second-largest) is the provincial capital. And, in a part of the country that is crazier about the CFL than any other professional sport, is also home to Rider Nation.

"Certainly, they've got the Saskatchewan Roughriders," Lubiniecki said, "and they like to let everyone know where they are stationed."

Having a CFL team stationed in your backyard would make anyone not within driving distance a tad jealous. But the reason why the Blades do not like the Pats (and vice versa) also has to do with the hockey.

"You always knew it was going to be a big night," said former Saskatoon Blades left winger Wendel Clark. "They were always exciting games."

Part of that reason was that throughout the years, both franchises have prescribed to the Brian Burke philosophy of building belligerent rosters. Skill was coveted. But players also had to have a barbed-wire temperament, as well as a willingness to get his hands dirty – if not bloody.

Just look at the some of the stars from those bygone eras: Grimson (484 penalty minutes in 182 games, Wendel Clark (478 PIMs in 136 games), Dave Brown (344 PIMs in 62 games), Leroy Gorski (747 PIMs in 163 games) Joey Kocur (547 PIMs in 131 games). Put those guys on the ice together at the same time and something bad was bound to happen.

"I remember playing one night and for whatever reason Wendel and I got into it," Grimson said. "That's when I really appreciated how tough he was. He probably conceded 20 to 30 pounds to me and about six inches.

"I hit him with a shot that dropped him to his knees. But before I could get another one in on him, he was back up and hitting me. I was like, 'what's going on?' But that was how it was back then. You would get a few licks in on them. And they would get you back. And on and on it went."

Indeed, years later that rivalry seems stronger. For that, Mike Reich can be thanked (or blamed). The native of Craik, Sask. — roughly in between Regina and Saskatoon — played for both teams during his junior career. And though Blades GM and coach Lorne Molleken said, "He was a pain in the ass to play against," Reich clearly picked sides.

While playing for Saskatoon, he received an eight-game suspension for allegedly eye-gouging a Regina player. Another time, he got tossed from a game after referees noticed that he had printed an offensive message on his stick. And Reich provided a *Slap Shot* moment when he attacked the Pats' bench before the puck could be dropped.

"They were still singing the National Anthem and the refs are taking him to the penalty box," Molleken laughed. "I remember when we had to trade him, he came to me and said, 'oh, trade me someplace where I can play Regina eight times.'

"Every game that he played against Regina, we knew, was going to be an adventure. You didn't know what he was going to do."

> "I hit him with a shot that dropped him to his knees. But before I could get another one in on him, he was back up and hitting me."
> - Stu Grimson on fighting Wendel Clark

You also did not know what the fans were going to do. While Saskatoon upgraded its arena in 1988, Regina still plays out of the intimate Brandt Centre, where fans sometimes get too close.

"They threw beer on us," Molleken said, "and they were right there down in the players' box almost. We've had our wars, certainly."

For Molleken, the war is personal. His family moved to Regina when he was 12 years old. And he has coached both teams at one point in time. But when he arrives to the city these days, he is the enemy.

"I spent a lot of time in Regina and I still do," Molleken said. "My family is still there. And I have lots of friends there. But it doesn't matter. I still hear cat-calls all the time, whether I'm in the arenas or walking on the streets."

VS. SEAN AVERY
THE NHL

Some people believe that Sean Avery and the NHL have been engaged in a ferocious battle since the day the tempestuous left winger played his first game in the league back in 2001.

That's true, but it sells short Avery's legendarily combative nature. In reality and throughout his career, it's always been Avery vs. The Whole of The Hockey World. And one story that dates back prior to the super pest's NHL days makes that fact perfectly clear.

The scene: the 1998 Ontario League All-Star Game in which Avery was playing. Matt Cooke, one of his opponents that night – and himself no on-ice angel – drilled Avery into the boards from behind, hitting him so hard that he had to be taken to hospital.

Avery's father, Al, told *SunMedia* in 2008 that Cooke "almost killed" Sean on the play. But there was no controversy that night, no candlelight vigil for Al's kid, no public groundswell demanding either retribution or atonement.

Let that sink in for a second. Avery was physically attacked by another player *at an all-star game.*

That might be the first-ever recorded incident of body contact at any all-star game in hockey history. But it was an indication of how loathed Avery was at such an early age – and how despised he continues to be to this day.

Even Sean Avery's smile could infuriate opponents.

Avery's troubles with teammates, coaches and the opposition probably had something to do with the fact he wasn't drafted out of junior hockey. Basically, he had to force himself on the NHL and dare teams to turn away his talents.

The Detroit Red Wings were the first to take a chance on Avery, signing him as an unrestricted free agent in 1999 and playing him in 75 games over two seasons (2001-2003). But Avery was shipped to Los Angeles at the 2003 trade deadline in the deal that sent Mathieu Schneider to Motown.

"Fatso didn't shake my hand." - Sean Avery goading Martin Brodeur

Five years after the deal, Detroit GM Ken Holland said he disposed of Avery for reasons that reverberated on and off the ice.

"Our concern was his lack of respect for the game, the people in the game," Holland told NHL.com. "With the Internet and as the way the world has evolved, especially since the early '90s, I think everybody wants positive publicity. I think what we're all looking for is positive publicity and I don't think that negative publicity is what we're looking for."

By the time he arrived in L.A., negative publicity and naked belligerence was beginning to be Avery's stock-in-trade. He led the league in penalty minutes (261) during the 2003-04 season; and during the 2004-05 lockout season, he accused the NHL Players' Association of lying to its membership.

Then, during the 2005-06 campaign, he again led the NHL in penalties – and also ramped up his rhetoric.

After French-Canadian Coyotes blueliner Denis Gauthier concussed Kings forward Jeremy Roenick with a check, Avery told reporters, "I think it was typical of most French guys in our league with a visor on, running around and playing tough and not backing anything up."

He later apologized for the remarks.

In addition, Oilers enforcer Georges Laraque alleged that Avery called him a 'monkey' (Avery has insisted he didn't use the word) during a game. And after being the first to be fined $1,000 by the league under new diving rules, Avery earned another $1,000 fine for criticizing league disciplinarian Colin Campbell.

Avery also couldn't avoid conflict with the media that season. Taking exception to comments Anaheim TV broadcaster (and former NHLer)

Brian Hayward made during a Kings/Ducks game a few days earlier, Avery called Hayward out in a dressing room showdown, calling him a "(crappy) announcer" and "crappy player."

Hayward struck a blow for Avery-haters everywhere when he responded, "How would you know? When I played, you were in your third year of eighth grade."

Avery also set new career highs in goals (15), assists (24) and points (39) that year. However, his act wore thin with the Kings – he was suspended by the organization after run-ins with coaches and disputes about his practice habits – and he was traded to the Rangers in February of 2007.

Some would argue Avery sparked the Blueshirts' improbable playoff run the rest of that season. But the Rangers themselves called Avery "not a mature player" and "a detriment to the team" in an arbitration hearing at the end of the season.

Avery shook off the Rangers' negotiating tactics – and a broken wrist – the next year to score 15 for the team. But it was in the first round of the 2008 playoffs that he would have one of his most memorable clashes with the league – and force it to create what's come to be known as "The Sean Avery Rule" on the spot.

Playing against New Jersey in Game 3 of their opening round series, Avery decided to stand facing Martin Brodeur and wave his stick in the Devils goalie's face. Nobody had ever seen a screening tactic like it before – and nobody in the league wanted to see it again.

Overnight, NHL brass decided they would award an unsportsmanlike conduct penalty to any player who replicated Avery's goalie-obstructing actions. Even then, however, they couldn't keep him from engaging in further acts of antagonism.

After the Rangers eliminated the Devils, Brodeur skated past Avery without acknowledging Avery's outstretched arm. When asked about it in a post-game scrum, Avery said, "Fatso didn't shake my hand."

It didn't come as a huge surprise to see Avery move on as an unrestricted free agent that summer. But again, he wasn't in his new home long before he immersed himself in controversy.

In November of 2008 – the first year of a four-year, $15.5-million contract with the Dallas Stars – Avery was alleged to have verbally assaulted a fan in Boston (the NHL investigated, but didn't suspend him).

And one month later, while in Calgary to play the Flames, he walked up to a group of reporters and began making indirect references to Elisha Cuthbert, a Hollywood actress and girlfriend of Calgary defenseman Dion Phaneuf.

> **"When I played, you were in your third year of eighth grade."**
> **- Brian Hayward mixing it up with Avery**

"I just want to comment on how it's become like a common thing in the NHL for guys to fall in love with my 'sloppy seconds,' " Avery said of Cuthbert, whom he dated prior to her relationship with Phaneuf. "I don't know what that's about."

That was the last straw for the NHL, which immediately suspended Avery indefinitely for behavior it called "unacceptable and antisocial.' His suspension was later set at six games, but in an unprecedented move, Avery was also made to undergo anger management treatment.

Yet that wasn't enough to make amends with his Stars teammates; they told management they didn't want him back on the roster under any circumstances, so co-GMs Brett Hull and Les Jackson first waived Avery – with no takers – then placed him on re-entry waivers, where he was claimed by the Rangers in March of 2009.

NORM GREEN
MINNESOTA

Perhaps the reason Norm Green was so reviled by fans of the Minnesota North Stars is because he was, at first, much admired. The Calgary businessman rode into town on a white horse, lassoing hearts before putting a bullet through them.

Mike Modano's North Stars were soon headed south to Dallas thanks to owner Norm Green.

"When Norm first came here in 1990 – and they went to the final in 1991 – he'd be up in a suite (in the Met Center) and fans would be bowing to him and waving," said Tom Reid, the former North Stars player and broadcaster who now does radio color for the Minnesota Wild. "He was like an emperor up there."

And the benevolent ruler told his subjects precisely what they wanted to hear. Their team, mired in turmoil for so long, was staying put.

"I have absolutely no interest in selling my team or moving it to another city," Green said in 1990. "Until our attendance improves we will continue to be involved in these rumors, but there's no possibility that they are correct."

Hallelujah, thought the faithful. Finally, a man with integrity and vision.

Less than two-and-a-half years later, the Stars were loading up the United moving vans, ready to high-tail it to Dallas.

> **"It's hard to believe we can't make it work in Minnesota, but we can make it work in Dallas."**
> **— Neal Broten**

And North Stars fans? Mention Green and they saw red.

"Fans were very upset when he took the team out of here," Reid said. "Their thought pattern when he took the team over in 1990 was that he was going to build this team into all kinds of things. When he took the team to Dallas, it really left a sour taste in the mouths of fans, the community and the former players who had made their home here."

Where did it all go wrong? How could a franchise playing in the hockey heartland of the United States move deep to the heart of...*Texas*? In 1993, the lake state had 2,141 registered hockey teams, 145 of them in high schools, 15 in colleges; they had 465 rinks state-wide and had sent 23 players to the NHL. By comparison, there were 58 hockey teams across the vast state of Texas, just four high school programs, none in college and a meagre 15 rinks. No Texan, at that point, had played a minute of NHL hockey.

"I remember going to Minnesota in 1978, thinking 'This is a Canadian city,' " said Bobby Smith, who had two tours of duty with the North Stars, including that final, fateful season. "It has way more in common with Calgary than many American cities."

On the surface the shift made little sense. But history shows us it made mucho dinero. The North Stars had bumped up attendance from about 6,000 in 1990 to roughly 15,000 in 1993, but ticket prices only fetched, on average, $21. Revenues were middling, with little hope – so it seemed – of much growth potential. And, in the wake of NHL salary disclosure, player expenses were soaring. Meantime, Green couldn't, or wouldn't, execute deals for an improved home or a more favorable lease. Throw in increased competition from the suddenly sexy Minnesota Timberwolves of the NBA, and big market Dallas and its lure of a greener financial picture, looked like the Promised Land.

"I think Norm made the determination that you couldn't make money in Minnesota with salaries going up and playing in an older building," Smith said. "Fans for so long had paid 1970s and 1980s prices. The idea of getting people to pay $120 for a center ice ticket wasn't going to happen."

Smith doesn't believe that it was Green's plan from the outset to buy low, for a reported $32 million, then high-tail it; rather circumstances changed and Green wasn't prepared to lose millions.

"He enjoyed being the majority owner," Smith said. "His personalized license plate read 'North Stars.' He watched practice and was in the office every day. I don't think he thought this was an opportunity to get his hands on a franchise and move it at the first opportunity.

"Anybody who's going to move a franchise, there's going to be a terrible backlash. And I don't recall any local guy willing to step up and say, 'Hey, if you're going to move the team I'll buy it and keep it in town.' "

Still, confusion and resentment reigned.

"It's hard to believe we can't make it work in Minnesota, but we can make it work in Dallas," Minnesota native and North Star mainstay Neal Broten told The Hockey News in '93. "But our owner has it set in his mind he's going to move the team and that's what he's going to do. He owns the team, he can do what he wants with it."

The North Stars supporters, who began calling the owner "Norm Greed," were a little more direct with their hard feelings. In the dying embers of the 1992-93 season, after Green had completed the deal to go south, fans at the Met Center united in their disdain for the owner. During breaks in play – back in a time when forced entertainment wasn't part of the game night experience – the crowd would take advantage of the pauses and fill the air with chants of "Norm Sucks!" The same slogan could be found on buttons and T-shirts.

"When he came here, he said, 'Only an idiot could lose money on hockey in Minnesota.' " Julie Hammond, president of the North Star booster club, told Sports Illustrated in a 1993 article. "Well, I guess he proved that point."

Reid recalls the anger being deep and widespread – so much so that Green became persona non grata in the northern state. Some have even called him the most hated man in Minnesota's history.

"I don't think Norm or his wife have ever been back to Minnesota."
- Tom Reid

"I don't think Norm or his wife have ever been back to Minnesota since they left," Reid said. "I've never seen him back here and I don't know why he'd want to come back here."

Compounding matters was a sexual harassment lawsuit filed against Green by his one-time executive assistant, Kari Dziedzic, that gave him yet another reason to leave town.

While Green's charms wore thin in Minnesota, they were embraced in Dallas, where he eventually flipped the team to Thomas Hicks for a reported $82 million, making a tidy profit in the process. Maybe it is easy being Green after all.

VS. COLORADO AVALANCHE
DETROIT RED WINGS

When people are asked to name the ry in pro sports in the late 1990s and early 2000s, they usually go right to the usual suspects: Red Sox-Yankees, Dodgers-Giants, Celtics-Lakers, Bears-Packers, Maple Leafs-Canadiens.

Not even close, none of them. Not to the rivalry, anyway, that was the Detroit Red Wings vs. Colorado Avalanche.

Some of the better rivalries in pro sports from about 1995-2002 or so had a nastiness quotient to approach that of the Wings-Avs, but when you combined the nastiness *plus* the high skill level from both teams involved, nothing really came close.
Consider a few facts:

- The Wings and Avalanche met in the Western Conference playoffs five out of six years, from 1996-2002, and the teams won a combined five

Stanley Cups overall in that span. Either Detroit or Colorado made it to the Western final in every one of those years.

- The rosters of the two teams from those years had 21 players who either already have made it to the Hockey Hall of Fame or are considered shoo-ins for future consideration.

- The skill players fought each other, the goalies fought, the goons fought, the fans fought and even members of the press from both cities nearly came to blows on more than one occasion.

It was hockey at its best played and ugliest. In other words: perfect.

"The more that time goes by, the more I keep looking at those years and thinking, 'Did that really happen?' " said Avalanche defenseman Adam Foote, who played in all the games from those years and has the scars to prove it. "It's hard to describe actually; the games were beyond intense. You felt like every single second was life or death in some way. Nothing felt better than beating them, and nothing felt worse than losing."

The thing about the Wings-Avs rivalry that makes it even more amazing: it probably never should have happened. If the province of Quebec hadn't been squeezed by a drop in the Canadian dollar and an escalation in player salaries in the mid-90s, the beloved Nordiques never would have moved to a city like Denver, which had previously been known as a failed NHL town when the Colorado Rockies moved to New Jersey in 1982. If the Red Wings themselves hadn't run up the score on an embarrassed Patrick Roy and the 1995 Montreal Canadiens in a Dec. 2, 1995, game at the old Forum, Roy never would have forced his own fiery exit in a trade four days later to the fledgling Avalanche. And

Detroit's Martin Lapointe and Colorado's Eric Messier duke it out in one of the numerous scraps between the two powerhouse teams in the 1990s.

if a feisty winger named Claude Lemieux hadn't absent-mindedly signed his name to a faxed contract offer late in the regular season of 1994-95 in New Jersey – shortly before winning the Conn Smythe Trophy, against the Wings – he never would have forced a trade to Colorado, either. In that case, two of the most central players of the great Detroit-Colorado rivalry never would have been on hand.

Another ironic fact of the rivalry: The Avalanche's first game in Denver – Oct. 6, 1995 – was a fairly placid affair, against Detroit. Seven months later, blood literally was splashing on the ice, and the hatred between the teams, fans and cities was real.

"It was probably the best rivalry I was ever a part of," said legendary Detroit coach Scotty Bowman, which is quite a statement in itself.

Most people remember Lemieux's vicious hit from behind on Detroit's Kris Draper in Game 6 of the '96 Western final as the touchstone to the intense rivalry, but many forget it actually started in Game 3, at the old McNichols Sports Arena in Denver.

> ## "Nothing felt better than beating them, and nothing felt worse than losing."
> ## – Adam Foote

On a play to the left half-boards in the Colorado end, Foote's head was driven into the glass by a sucker punch from Detroit's Slava Kozlov, opening an 18-stitch gash on his forehead. A few minutes later, Lemieux drilled Kozlov with a sucker punch of his own, which led to his being suspended for Game 4.

On the way out of McNichols after Game 3, with his wife and infant son in tow, Lemieux walked past the idling Red Wings team bus, when suddenly he heard a shout from inside.

"Hey Lemieux, you son of a bitch, I hope they suspend your ass," Bowman yelled.

"Excuse me?" said Lemieux, who instantly recognized the voice as belonging to Bowman. Lemieux went so far as to step inside the bus to confront Bowman and was greeted with numerous further shouts of profanity from Bowman and Red Wings players, still savoring the 6-4 victory which had closed their series deficit at that point to 2-1.

When Colorado came home with a 3-2 lead for Game 6, Lemieux early on ran Draper head-first into the boards, resulting in multiple facial fractures and blood all over the ice by the Wings bench. Lemieux, who would be suspended for the first two games of the Stanley Cup final against Florida for the hit, seemed to shrug off the hit as an innocent act, which only inflamed the Red Wings and their fans – who hadn't tasted Stanley Cup success since 1955 – even further.

"I can't believe I shook his freakin' hand," said Detroit's Dino Ciccarelli after the game, in one of the more memorable quotes of the rivalry.

Detroit vowed revenge on Colorado, but entering a March 26, 1997 game at Joe Louis Arena, the Avs were not only the defending Stanley Cup champs, they were dominating the Western Conference again. Detroit seemed old and tired next to an Avs team that featured Roy and numerous other stars such as Lemieux, Foote, Peter Forsberg, Joe Sakic, Adam Deadmarsh, Sandis Ozolinsh and Valeri Kamensky.

But starting with that memorable night and continuing for the next two years, bragging rights in the rivalry belonged to Detroit. A brash, rugged third-line forward named Darren McCarty saw an opportunity to exact physical revenge on Lemieux during a stop in action late in the first period, and get revenge he did, pummeling Lemieux with a flurry of punches that left the veteran Avs winger dazed and bloodied on the ice, with hands over head in meek defense.

That started a wild donnybrook that saw Roy and veteran Wings goalie Mike Vernon trade blows at center ice, a rare fight between goalies that left Roy with a bloody face. When McCarty – whom referee Paul Devorski would later admit should have been tossed from the game for cold-cocking Lemieux unprovoked – scored the winning goal on Roy in overtime to cap a 6-5 comeback win, The Joe went wild. The Wings seemed like a new team after that, winning the next two Stanley Cups, while Colorado sagged from the affair.

"It changed the complexion of our team in the dressing room," McCarty said. "We were kind of getting the reputation at the time around the league of a team that was too pretty and not gritty enough. After that game, we felt like we could play any kind of style and still win games." The Avs remained defiant, with veteran Mike Keane mocking Detroit for only fighting on Joe Louis ice, calling the Wings "a bunch of homers." In the '97 Western final in the waking moments of a blowout loss in

Game 4, Avs coach Marc Crawford launched into a blisteringly profane tirade at Bowman – even mocking the metal plate he supposedly had in his head from a junior hockey accident (Bowman never had a plate inserted).

"My stomach still churns whenever I see that Detroit logo."
- Mike Keane

Bowman responded with a simple "I knew your father before you did," referring to Crawford's dad, Floyd, a longtime coach. Crawford only responded with more profanity.

"Yeah, and he thinks you're a (bleeping bleep) too," Crawford said.

Detroit went on to win the Cup in '97 and '98, with Roy and Detroit goalie Chris Osgood having another fight at center ice in an April, '98 game in Detroit: The Wings seemed well on their way to a third Cup in a row after taking a 2-0 Western Conference semifinal lead on the Avs in 1999. The first two wins came on Denver ice, and workers from Detroit-based Northwest Airlines greeted the Avs' charter plane prior to Game 3 with mocking sweeps of their broomsticks. This time, the Avalanche would fight back.

Colorado suddenly awoke with a blizzard of goal-scoring on three different Wings goalies in sweeping the next four games. The Avs followed that up with probably the rivalry's most lopsided series victory, a five-game triumph in a 2000 conference semi-final match.

After Colorado won the Cup in 2001, all the bragging rights to the rivalry were back in Denver's camp. And when the great Colorado center Forsberg scored in overtime to beat Detroit in Game 5 the '02 Western final, the Avs had a 3-2 lead heading back to the Pepsi Center. One more win, and it would be four out of five playoff series in Colorado's favor against Detroit. The '97 series would be just an aberration.

But what made the rivalry so great was one side's ability to reach back and land a great punch when all seemed lost. Detroit, behind goalie Dominik Hasek, shut out the Avs in the final two games – with the deciding Game 7 a 7-0 blowout in Detroit.

Today, players from both sides speak in reverent terms of what it was like during the rivalry, calling it the best hockey they were ever a part of. But still, not all animosity has died away.

"My stomach still churns whenever I see that Detroit logo," Keane said.

SPRAGUE CLEGHORN
EDDIE GERARD

VS.

Sprague Cleghorn had a very different persona than former teammate Eddie Gerard.

To his admirers, Eddie Gerard, captain of the Ottawa Senators when the team won the Stanley Cup three times in four seasons from 1920-23, was a natural.

"He was one of the greatest men the game has known," former Ottawa manager Tommy Gorman once told the *Globe & Mail*.

To his detractors, Sprague Cleghorn caused natural disasters of epic proportions.

"He was ready, willing and eager to swing fists or stick, at any time," Gorman said, assessing Cleghorn's hockey strategy to the Ottawa *Citizen*.

Together they were dynamite, the first great defense pairing in NHL history. Even though this duo was anything but two of a kind – and rarely kind to each other.

The rivalry between Gerard and Cleghorn developed because they were polar opposites in personality and in their perception of how the game should be played.

"Gerard didn't always like Sprague's freewheeling ways," wrote Baz O'Meara of the Montreal *Star*.

An original Hockey Hall of Famer in 1945, Gerard carried himself with class and deportment.

"As a competitor and in the years after he had retired from active competition, (Gerard) earned a reputation for sportsmanship of the highest order," the *Globe & Mail* noted upon his death in 1937. Following his playing days, Gerard served on the NHL rules committee.

During his playing days, Cleghorn served to rage against said rulebook. "Sprague used to test every guy who came into the league," the Montreal *Gazette*'s Dink Carroll wrote. "Two-handers across the ankles as soon as the guy came into the slot."

According to some reports, Marie Evelyn Moreton, wife of the Viscount Byng of Vimy, was so appalled by the work of Cleghorn that she donated the Lady Byng Trophy in 1924 to encourage sportsmanlike play.

It wasn't merely his roguish ways between the boards that left Gerard unimpressed, though. Off the ice, Cleghorn went equally out of bounds. A notorious womanizer, Cleghorn was divorced twice. Sidelined by a fractured leg in 1918, Cleghorn was arrested for assaulting his wife with his crutch.

The grounds for Evelyn Cleghorn's divorce were explained in a July 29, 1921 New York *Times* article. "A chance visit of Mrs. Evelyn Cleghorn to Ottawa…not only located her missing husband…but revealed the fact that he was living there with another woman whom he introduced as his wife."

"Sprague used to test every guy who came into the league." – Dink Carroll

Traded to Montreal in 1921, Cleghorn promised fireworks when the Canadiens came to Ottawa for a Feb. 1, 1922 game. He delivered, putting three Senators out of commission, including his old partner.

"Gerard received an ugly gash over the eye and was removed to hospital for treatment," the *Globe* reported. Ottawa sought Cleghorn's permanent expulsion from the NHL, but was denied.

Gerard turned to coaching after his playing days were cut short by a throat ailment, leading the Montreal Maroons to the 1926 Stanley Cup. Cleghorn coached the Maroons in 1931-32, but was let go after one season. According to author Trent Frayne's book, *The Mad Men Of Hockey*, team discipline was a major problem and Cleghorn was known for sneaking women into his berth on the train during road trips.

According to O'Meara, later in life the two men patched up their differences during an encounter at a golf course.

"Let's not be foolish any longer," Cleghorn reportedly said to Gerard. "You were the greatest player on defense I ever played with."

After shaking hands, Gerard countered, "You were pretty good, too."

VS. UNIVERSITY OF MICHIGAN
MICHIGAN STATE UNIVERSITY

It's Friday night at Munn Ice Arena in East Lansing, Mich., and it's loud. Thousands of fans scream from the stands as the hometown Michigan State Spartans skate onto the ice. The cheers turn to boos when the visiting team, the University of Michigan Wolverines, hits the ice.

It's typical for nearby communities to have storied battles. But the rivalry between the University of Michigan and Michigan State University – dubbed the 'Backyard Brawl' – is one of the most intense in the game.

Both schools regularly produce NHL stars and are highly regarded teams, but that's not the only reason.

In 2009-10, Andrew Rowe was a junior and the alternate captain of the Spartans and called the rivalry a "piggyback through history."

"It's been a rivalry since both teams started," he said. "It's always been a big rivalry. It goes beyond even hockey – it's like we're the little sister and they're the big brother or vice versa."

Chris Summers, the captain of the Wolverines and a Phoenix Coyotes draft pick, agreed.

"It's been a distinguished, hard-fought battle over a lot of years," he said. "It's a rivalry like no other. It's more emotional than any other game we play."

The schools are only about 45 minutes apart and both have prestigious, championship-winning teams. Players on each team always seem to know each other, which makes the battle a little more personal, Summers noted.

> **"We looked around and couldn't even hear each other talk, it was so loud."**
> **– Andrew Rowe**

The teams also play each other annually at Joe Louis Arena – home of the Detroit Red Wings – in a battle for state supremacy. On Oct. 6, 2001, the teams squared off in the 'Cold War' game – an outdoor match that set the world record for the largest crowd at an ice hockey game.

54

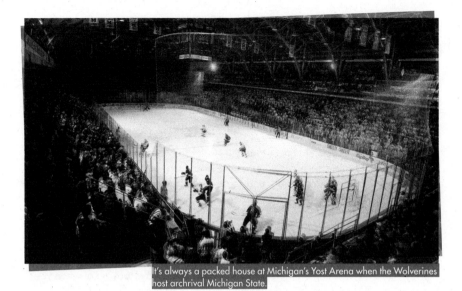

It's always a packed house at Michigan's Yost Arena when the Wolverines host archrival Michigan State.

That night, 74,544 fans packed Spartan Stadium (the home of MSU's football team) to 103.4 percent capacity and watched the Spartans and Wolverines skate to a 3-3 tie after an intense game.

"It was a surreal experience," said Montreal Canadiens center Mike Cammalleri, who played in that game for Michigan. "It was at a football stadium, there was tailgating, it was full of the tradition that both schools have and it was just a lot of fun."

The sheer attendance at games between MSU and Michigan should expose how much energy this rivalry gives off.

Rowe knows first-hand how much power the crowd at games between Michigan and Michigan State can bring. In his freshman year, he was a scratch for an away game and was sitting in the stands with a friend at Michigan's legendary Yost Arena. Michigan State was up 1-0 with five minutes remaining.

"I looked at my buddy," Rowe recalled, "and we looked around, and couldn't even hear each other talk, it was so loud. The place was erupting even though they were losing."

Summers said the game they played in '09-10 at Joe Louis Arena was an especially good example of their rivalry.

"We were up by three goals, then they made a huge comeback and took the lead," he said. "It was amazing back-and-forth hockey for the rest of the game."

Detroit Red Wings left winger Drew Miller spent three seasons playing on the Michigan State squad after dreaming about playing for the Spartans as a youth.

"Even as a kid I could see the rivalry between the two teams," he said. "I remember watching the two teams play and being so happy when Michigan State won, and so devastated when they lost."

Miller, who played at State along with his brother, Ryan – Buffalo's star netminder – says the intensity of the rivalry is also because the teams play each other so often.

"When the schedule came out, you were always looking at when you'd play Michigan and start gearing up right away," he said. "Every time we played them, the whole week leading into the game was planning. It was more exciting than playing any other team."

But Cammalleri knows that no matter how much planning goes into it, one team is always going to come out on top and sometimes embarrassment is inevitable. In his sophomore year, he was playing against Michigan State on enemy ice. As the announcers called his name, he took two strides forward and fell flat on the ice.

"The crowd gave me a standing ovation, but they weren't clapping for me, they were laughing," he recalled. "They literally wouldn't stop until I got up and gave them a salute.

"It was probably the most embarrassing game of my hockey career."

"When the schedule came out, you were always looking at when you'd play Michigan and start gearing up right away."
- Drew Miller

PHILADELPHIA PHANTOMS
HERSHEY BEARS

VS.

Separated by a hundred miles of Pennsylvania countryside, the Hershey Bears and Philadelphia Phantoms already had the first and arguably most important ingredient in building any rivalry: proximity. They met a dozen times during the regular season in all but one of their 13-year co-existence in the American League that ended in 2009.

But, in this case, geography merely played a supporting role. The true contempt between players, management and cities began before the teams played even a single game.

No quarter was given nor expected between the American League's Phantoms and Bears.

The Phantoms were the fourth reincarnation of AHL hockey in Philadelphia, starting with the Ramblers, who played for the AHL's predecessor, the International-American League, from 1936 to 1941. They were followed by the Rockets (1941-42 and 1946-49) and Firebirds (1977-79).

Hershey, too, can trace its lineage back to the IAHL days, having begun play in 1938. In their 72-year history, the Bears won 2,544 of 5,291 regular season games and 10 Calder Cup championships – all league records.

"It was quite a rivalry," said Bill Barber, a Hall of Fame winger for the Philadelphia Flyers who coached the Phantoms in each of their first four seasons, after finishing the 1995-96 campaign behind the Hershey bench.

"I'll tell ya, it was a war zone every time we played. More old-time hockey than you could ever imagine. Heated? I mean, it was unbelievable. There wasn't any one game that I can remember when we played Hershey that there wasn't a confrontation. Always."

In 1996, the Flyers moved into a new state-of-the-art facility, the CoreStates Center, located just across the parking lot from the Spectrum, their home since the NHL expanded to 12 teams in 1967. With their original building empty, the Flyers organization chose to fill it by moving their AHL farm team out of Hershey, where it had played since 1984.

"I think that was the start of it," Barber said. He replaced Jay Leach as coach of the Bears midway through the 1995-96 season and moved with the team to Philadelphia, giving him the distinction of being the last Hershey coach under the Flyers regime and the first of the new Phantoms.

"I think what happened was maybe Hershey was disappointed that we had taken our players and opened up our own franchise in Philly. And, knowing the players that were playing in Hershey were now playing in Philly, and they had had a good rapport with the Hershey community, I think the rivalry really started there. It ended up to be quite a rivalry, to say the least."

To replace the Flyers, Hershey welcomed in the defending Stanley Cup-champion Colorado Avalanche as its NHL affiliate. The Avs prospects were quite familiar to Bears fans; as the Cornwall Aces, they had eliminated Hershey in the playoffs two of the previous three years.

"When you beat a team two times out of three in the playoffs, you're going to create a rivalry," said Bob Hartley. An assistant in Cornwall in 1993-94, he was the Aces' coach from 1994-96 and came with the team to Hershey for its first two seasons.

"We were the big enemies and suddenly we move into Hershey and it was like the rivals invaded the city. Philly was building a new rink and they decided to leave Hershey, and there was turmoil between the Hershey management and the Flyers management."

Part of that stemmed from a goodwill gesture extended by the Hershey officials to their future players and staff.

"In our final visit of the regular season when we were in Cornwall, the Hershey management as a token of appreciation or maybe of welcome for the upcoming year, they had put pizza on our bus to go back to Cornwall," Hartley said. "I guess that the coaching staff of Hershey, who were paid by the Flyers, were made aware of this and obviously that created a big fuss. There was lots of turmoil."

When the teams finally met on the ice in a 1996-97 exhibition game, the results were inevitable. Numerous fights and penalties made the afternoon game so long that the NHL pre-season game played that night had to have its start delayed.

"There were fights every 10 seconds," Hartley said. "It was like a demolition derby out there."

Hershey and Philadelphia met 10 times during the 1996-97 season. Though the Bears had a 5-3-2 series advantage, the Phantoms won the Mid-Atlantic Division with 111 points, 10 more than Hershey.

"When I walked in with the rest of my players from Cornwall and the Colorado prospects, the rivalry was already started," Hartley said. "At the start of the year, my new boss, Jay Feaster, who was vice-president and GM of the team, told me, 'Listen, you can lose every game in the season but, please, win the games against Philly.' I knew right then that we were in for a treat."

> **"I'll tell ya, it was a war zone every time we played. More old-time hockey than you could ever imagine."**
> **- Bill Barber**

The new-old rivals would meet again in the second round of the Calder Cup playoffs, an epic seven-game series that went to Hershey, which went on to win the Calder Cup in its first season under the new affiliation.

But a 7-4 Phantoms win in Game 2 earned an entry into the AHL record book as having the most single-game penalty minutes in post-season history. The marathon contest featured 14 game misconducts that resulted in a pair of suspensions and the rare use of five different goaltenders.

"I don't know how many fights there were, but I know one thing. We didn't win one," Hartley said. "J-F Labbe was my No. 1 goalie and I told him, 'I'm sorry, you have a pulled groin.' I tell the ref that I had to pull him out of the game and dress my third (string) goalie and five minutes after this, a brawl broke out, (Philly netminder) Neil Little crossed the ice and beat the crap out of Sinuhe Wallinheimo, and he was beaten so bad I had to put my third goalie in to finish the game."

Philadelphia got its scoreboard revenge in 1997-98, finishing first in the division again and sweeping Hershey in four second round games en route to its second Calder Cup title.

"It was hard-nosed hockey," Barber said. "They had muscle in their lineup, we had muscle in our lineup. They had gritty players, we had

> **"There were fights every 10 seconds. It was like a demolition derby out there."**
> **- Bob Hartley**

gritty players. They had good goaltending, we had good goaltending. It was unreal how everything materialized."

Hershey won both of the other playoff series with Philadelphia, in 2000 and 2009, including a 1-0 victory on April 24, 2009 in their final meeting ever.

Other than the Phantoms' 16-game win streak against Hershey that lasted from Nov. 2, 2003 to Nov. 27. 2004, the two teams were evenly matched. In 154 regular season games, Philadelphia won 74, the Bears 72. They were separated in the standings by nine or fewer points six times.

When they met, the teams averaged 9,718 fans per game, a total of 1,496,610 people: 851,456 in Philadelphia, and 645,154 in Hershey, which moved from Hersheypark Arena to a more spacious Giant Center in 2002.

"We sold the buildings out for a reason," Barber said. "It was almost like a war game. I'm going to tell you something, it was tough hockey. It was a lot of fun to coach and be involved in, believe me. There was no room to have an evening off, I can assure you of that."

Of all the characters from both teams, perhaps the most flamboyant and popular was rugged winger Frank 'The Animal' Bialowas. At 6-foot and 235 pounds, he had 12 goals and 555 penalty minutes in 156 games for the Phantoms from 1996-99, and skated in 40 games for Hershey in 1999-2000, with four goals and 65 PIM.

"We would go on the road and we would sell buildings out because 'The Animal' was in our lineup," Barber said. "He had the long hair, he was tough as nails and when he was in the lineup you knew something was going to happen. And the truth of it all, he was a very coachable guy, a great guy."

Hartley went on to coach the Avalanche and Atlanta Thrashers from 1998-2007, but continues to cherish his part in the AHL's greatest rivalry.

"Me and Billy Barber were going at it every game," he said. "Bialowas was coming to do his 100 push-ups right on the red line, yapping at our players. Both managements were not even looking at each other. It was a war off the ice, it was a war on the benches, it was a war on the ice. I think it made for very interesting games."

SOVIET UNION
CZECHOSLOVAKIA

Soviet and Czechoslovak teams had a fierce rivalry in the 1950s and early 1960s, one which reached a peak after the invasion of Soviet tanks to quell a political uprising against communism in August of 1968.

Making things worse, Czechoslovakia was supposed to host the 1969 World Championship, but had to pull out because of the invasion. The result was a literal war on ice that lasted for more than a decade.

When the two countries met in Stockholm in the spring of 1969, the Czechoslovaks came on to the ice with fire in their eyes and beat the defending World and Olympic champion Soviets twice, 2-0 and 4-3.

Czechoslovak star Jaroslav Holik rubbed salt in the emotional wounds of Soviet goaltender Viktor Zinger after his team's first goal, poking his stick repeatedly at Zinger's face and calling him a "bloody communist."

Team captain Josef Golonka displayed his feelings towards the Soviets by converting his hockey stick into a pretend rifle.

"We said to ourselves, even if we have to die on the ice, we have to beat them," said Golonka in an interview many years later.

Before the first game, some Czechoslovak players had defied the Communist Party by covering up the red star on their jersey with tape. The star pledged allegiance to the USSR.

Soviet winger Evgeny Zimin remembered the game during an interview in Moscow in 1989 for Lawrence Martin's book, *The Red Machine*.

"The integrity of the Czechoslovak players and their pride was on the line," he said. "They decided that if they couldn't beat us with tanks, then they could beat us on the ice rinks."

The pot was still boiling three years later when Vaclav Nedomansky fired a puck into the Soviet bench at the 1972 Olympics in Japan. The Soviets won that gold medal with a 5-2 win.

However, the Czechoslovaks exacted revenge on home ice in Prague just two months later, upsetting the Olympic champions 3-2 to win the gold medal at the 1972 World Championship, snapping a nine-year Soviet run.

> "We said to ourselves, even if we have to die on the ice, we have to beat them."
> - Josef Golonka

In April of 1967 – more than a year before the Soviet invasion – Stepan Chervonenko, the Soviet ambassador to Czechoslovakia, had sent a top-secret cable to Moscow. He recommended serious consideration be given to halting matches between the two countries in Czechoslovak territory and not sending Soviet officials to work games involving Czechoslovakia in the future.

The Czechoslovakians got the upper hand in this 1968 Olympic tilt, but the battle with the Soviets was always hot.

When Czechoslovakia stunned the Soviets 5-4 at the 1968 Olympics in France, fans back home in Prague scribbled the final score on streets, walls and kiosks in a show of defiance.

At the 1985 World Championship, a 2-1 win over the Soviets in the medal round was a stepping stone to the gold for Czechoslovakia, which beat Canada and Mario Lemieux 5-3 on the final day.

From the day the two countries first met at a World Championship in 1954 until the 1992 Olympics, the Soviets posted an overall record of 37-12-8 against Czechoslovakia, but the perennial world champs earned very few of their wins without paying a heavy price physically.

During the same 38-year period, the Soviets once went undefeated against Sweden for 47 consecutive games. Canada, represented by players from the NHL, beat the Soviets only once between 1977 and 1992.

But as hot as the rivalry was, there were occasions when the Soviets did favors for the Czechoslovaks whom, despite the political turmoil, they considered their Slavic brothers. At the 1982 World Championship in Finland, the Soviets clinched the gold medal early and Canada was in line to take the silver if the Soviets defeated Czechoslovakia on the final day.

It has never been proven, but many observers believe the Soviets tanked the final game, which ended in a 0-0 tie, so that the Czechoslovaks would get a point and earn the silver ahead of Canada.

At one point in the game, it is said, Sergei Makarov had a clear-cut break-away, but instead of shooting, circled back into the neutral zone with the puck.

Recalling the game in an atmosphere free of government sanctions 20 years later, Soviet center Viktor Zhluktov would only say: "I guess we can talk about those things now, can't we!"

VS. BILL WIRTZ
CHICAGO

It's hard to find anyone who believes Bill Wirtz's policy not to televise Chicago Blackhawks home games was a good idea, but there was at least one occasion when it absolutely worked to his advantage.

March 19, 1998, was Denis Savard jersey retirement night at the United Center and Wirtz, as team owner, wanted to pay homage to his former superstar with a speech and ceremony at center ice. But as Wirtz stepped onto the red carpet and approached the podium, the boos began to cascade from the crowd – and they didn't stop until he made his exit.

"They booed him off the ice," remembered long-time Chicago hockey writer Matt Carlson. "He didn't even say a word. It was over the top. And he just walked off in disgrace."

While video of the spectacle doesn't reside on YouTube or anywhere else on the Internet – likely a result of Wirtz's no-home-TV policy – it was by all accounts a night to remember and a night to forget.

"That was inappropriate," said former Blackhawks goalie and broadcast-er, Darren Pang, who was in attendance that evening as a fan. "Savard was someone near and dear to Bill Wirtz. That wasn't a night to boo him."

And so it went with Wirtz. Hawks fans and those on the outside detested the man widely referred to as 'Dollar' Bill. They blamed him for squeezing his wallet and allowing Bobby Hull to flee to the WHA in 1972 (though many believe it was his father and owner at the time, Arthur Wirtz, who called the shots). They held him responsible for the franchise's epic Stanley Cup drought, which reached 46 years by the time of his death in 2007. But mostly, they reviled him for not airing home games in the local market.

Conversely, those employed by Wirtz saw a different side, a fiercely faithful boss who'd take care of his own. Talk to people who played on or managed his teams and virtually to a man they speak with reverence. To wit:

Michel Goulet, Hall of Famer and Blackhawks left winger from 1990-94: "I loved the man…sometimes people have a bad reputation, but I don't really listen to that. I want to find out on my own."

Recently deceased owner Bill Wirtz was blamed for many of Chicago's ills during his reign.

Rick Dudley, a consultant and assistant GM in Chicago from 2004-2009: "I thought he was a wonderful guy. He was a kind-hearted man who would do anything for you. He was one of the most loyal people I will ever know."

And Pang, a goalie for the club in the 1980s: "He was so loyal you could actually screw up two or three times and he'd still stand by you."

Pang credits Wirtz with helping him land on his feet, figuratively and literally, when his playing days abruptly ended in 1989. The netminder sustained a career-killing knee injury and knew his insurance claim was no slam-dunk. That's when Wirtz intervened and ensured all the paperwork was in order to secure Pang's short-term financial future. He also extended a broadcasting job to Pang and made certain his employee, who had a newborn son with medical issues, didn't lose any health coverage.

> "We quickly discovered that making fun of Bill Wirtz was a great way to get a response from the fans."
> - Mark Weinberg

"I remember a man who really wanted to help me out," Pang said. "And Bill Wirtz was true to his word."

But for every employee who fondly recalls their benign dictator, there are thousands of fans that only saw a cheap tyrant. Frustration that had simmered for years bubbled more ferociously after 1991, when Mark Weinberg started publishing the satirical, unofficial game program, *Blue Line*.

At first, Weinberg wanted to work with the Blackhawks, complementing the magazine the team sold on game nights with a stats-filled, pre-game analysis package. Upon pitching the idea to the club, Weinberg says he was summarily dismissed. "They told me to get lost," he said.

Instead, he went solo and started distributing the four-page newsletter outside the arena, filling it with biting satire and scathing editorial cartoons, much of it aimed at Wirtz. Weinberg's dissension landed him a trespassing arrest and a four-hour stint in jail. That's when he really amped things up.

"We quickly discovered that making fun of Bill Wirtz was a great way to get a response from the fans," Weinberg said. "But we weren't cutting edge. Bill Wirtz was already reviled. You can't successfully satirize someone who is beloved. We were just being reactive. But we were ruthless."

The negative Wirtz legacy snowballed and it became *de rigeur* in Chicago – a city renowned for loathing its sports teams owners – to put the Hawks owner at the top of their hate list. ESPN pegged him as the third greediest owner in sports in 2002; two years later, the network ranked Wirtz's franchise as the worst in all of sports. Even in death Wirtz wasn't safe from derision. After his passing, GM Dale Tallon gave a memorial speech at United Center and catcalls and boos bounced around the arena.

Video of that episode, incidentally, can be found on YouTube, most probably because the Hawks started airing homes games after he died. For Wirtz, it always comes back to home TV.

So why the policy? Ironically enough, the quality that so endeared him to people in his inner circle was at the heart of fans biggest source of disdain: loyalty. His dad, Arthur, owned many of America's arenas in the 1950s and firmly believed home TV would have a detrimental impact on attendance. Bill inherited his father's beliefs, or at least remained true to them, until the bitter end. It was joked that if Bill Wirtz ever aired home games, his dad would come out of the grave and spank him.

In addition, Wirtz put a high value on his regular customers.

"He believed that he was being true to the season-ticket subscribers," Pang said. "They weren't season-ticket holders, he always used the phrase 'subscribers.' Why should other people get to watch it at home for free when (the subscribers) have paid their money?"

But Pang recognizes why the policy left the masses alienated. He got to witness it first-hand with his seven-year-old son, who wanted to see his local heroes on TV, but couldn't. So he wrote a letter to the owner.

"I remember it," Pang said. "It went, 'My dad used to play for you, he was a goalie, we love hockey and now my favorite team is the Detroit Red Wings because we can't watch you on TV.'

"We never got a response."

On the ice, Chicago came close to glory a few times under Wirtz, enjoying success in the early 1990s, highlighted by a Stanley Cup final appearance in 1992. At the same time, the club had bitter partings with players such as Savard, Jeremy Roenick and Eddie Belfour.

While the feuds were often about money, it would be inaccurate to say Wirtz was always unwilling to spend. He was on record as saying he never took a dividend from the Hawks; that all profit was put back into the product. And significant signings – Doug Gilmour, $18 million over three years and Nikolai Khabibulin, $27 million over four – speak to that philosophy. Dudley says the management team he was part of with GM Dale Tallon was never shackled.

> **"They booed him off the ice. He didn't even say a word."**
> **- Matt Carlson**

"When Dale asked me to talk about a player or an acquisition and I went to Bill Wirtz, I don't think he ever turned us down," Dudley recalled. "And what's unfair, terribly unfair, is that everybody associates this big Chicago turnaround (in the late 2000s) with Bill and Bob (Pulford) not being there. It had started long before that. The day they hired Dale Tallon is when that started, and Bob Pulford was still the president and Bill Wirtz was still the owner. They began the process."

Fair or not, it's reality. The fans, for the most part, haven't forgiven. But we're not sure Wirtz would mind.

"Wirtz often said he put family first, business second and nothing else third," Weinberg said. "That included the fans."

MONTREAL CANADIENS
QUEBEC NORDIQUES

The Montreal Canadiens are coming out ahead in the 'Battle of Quebec' these days, but not without a fight.

The Nordiques may have left Quebec City after the 1994-95 NHL season, but the duel for provincial bragging rights is still waged on a regular basis in the form of alumni games that attract upwards of 15,000 fans.

Most games that feature players from past eras amount to nothing more than a lazy skate to stir up some memories for both the people on the ice and in the stands.

That, however, isn't always the case when the old Nords and Habs have at it. Jacques Demers, who coached both clubs during his long career, recalled one alumni game where, as bench boss of the Habs, he had to speak with his Quebec counterpart, Michel Bergeron, after things started spiraling out of control.

"Two years ago (in 2008) we played – this is true – the Montreal old-timers against the Nordiques old-timers," Demers said. "After the first period, I had to talk to Michel Bergeron. I said, 'Michel, we can't go on like this.'

La Belle Province was anything but when the Canadiens and Nordiques tangled.

"It was getting chippy. These guys who played 15 years ago…(the emotion) stayed."

Michel Goulet was one of those guys. The man who hit the 50-goal barrier in four consecutive seasons with the Nords said those old feelings of animosity never go completely dormant and require only a couple bumps in the corner to bloom once again.

> **"Gord Donnelly cracked a vertebrae in my back, he cross-checked me so hard behind the net one time." - Brian Hayward**

"It was just one of those things where a couple hits happen and Jacques and Michel had to be like, 'Calm down, guys. We all have to work tomorrow,' " Goulet said.

When it comes to Montreal consistently claiming the games that get played now, there's an intrinsic trouble for the former Nordiques.

"The problem we face is for the last 15 years we have the same 20 guys getting older and Montreal is getting younger all the time," Goulet laughed.

As for the games that really mattered, they were among the most intense ever witnessed in hockey. Don't let memories of firewagon hockey or the skill of Goulet and Peter Stastny fool you; these games were as much about toughness and intimidation as finesse and skill. For every soft pass by a Stastny brother or Mats Naslund, there was a menacing hack or whack coming from the likes of Chris Chelios and Dale Hunter. Former Habs goalie Brian Hayward doesn't need to put his pads back on to recall the fierce nature of Montreal-Quebec collisions.

"I have a constant reminder of the rivalry," Hayward said. "Gord Donnelly cracked a vertebrae in my back, he cross-checked me so hard behind the net one time.

"He almost folded me in half – it still hurts to this day."

There are a lot of layers to the conflict between the Canadiens and Nordiques, starting with the fact Montreal is a cosmopolitan city that has played host to major events such as Expo '67 and the 1976 Summer

Olympics. It also houses a hockey team that has set the gold standard for success in the NHL.

Quebec City is the provincial capital, but it's a smaller center that rarely attracts the world's attention on a large scale. That's why it was such a validating moment when the Nordiques joined the NHL from the defunct World Hockey Association.

"The Quebec Nordiques fans, they had been waiting and hoping to get an NHL team, so the young generation fell in love with them," Demers said.

Having their own entry in the world's best hockey league also offered people associated with the Nordiques – even a genuine Montreal boy like Demers – a chance to use hockey sticks as a means to carve out a niche of their own.

"When I went to the Nordiques, that's how I felt," Demers said. "Screw you guys, we're the Nordiques, we're going to do something good with this."

Added Goulet: "It was a typical, smaller town beside the big town."

Demers coached the Nords during their last two WHA seasons and their first campaign in the NHL, 1979-80. He said Montreal initially welcomed Quebec City under the banner of the fleur-de-lis and provincial pride.

But that all changed in 1982, when the clubs met for the first time in the playoffs. The heavily-favored Habs fell in a best-of-five first round series that went the distance, with Hunter scoring the overtime winner in the decisive game.

"I really believe the rivalry started there on that playoff game and series," Goulet said. "After that, Montreal was paying a bit more attention to our team."

Like all great rivalries, the hatred between Montreal and Quebec City was accentuated by consistent playoff skirmishes. The teams met in the post-season on four occasions between 1982 and 1987, each claiming two series apiece.

The rubber match came in 1993, after the Nords had resurrected their franchise with a number of high draft picks through some very lean years.

Quebec jumped out to a 2-0 series lead by opening with two wins at home, setting the stage for a very anxious scene in Montreal.

"It was hell. It was really hell," Demers said. "I could sense the tension... it's like everybody is whispering in my ear, 'You can't lose this series.' "

Demers said Habs GM Serge Savard was hearing even worse things from somebody who was taking the rivalry way too far.

"When we were down 0-2 somebody called my GM, Serge Savard, with some threats and Serge, who's a very calm man, said to me, 'Stay around me; there's something going on.' " Demers said. "He didn't get into too many details."

The Canadiens stormed back to win the series in six games and went on to claim the Stanley Cup that spring, thanks largely to the goaltending of Patrick Roy.

Three years later, Roy was tending goal for a Cup-winning Colorado Avalanche team that moved to Denver from his hometown of Quebec City after the 1995 season.

Hockey historians have always debated whether or not the Habs would have moved Roy to that franchise had it remained in Quebec. According to Roy, Montreal would have traded him to their oldest rival before ever shipping him up the highway to the Nordiques.

"Nope," replied Roy flatly when asked if the Canadiens would have considered trading him to Quebec. "The reason why I'm saying no to you is simple: It's because at the time (Habs GM) Rejean Houle told me he would not trade me in the same conference as Montreal.

"The teams that I heard of at the time were Chicago, Toronto and Colorado."

"Screw you guys, we're the Nordiques, we're going to do something good with this."
- Jacques Demers

NHL
WHA

VS.

Stars such as Gordie Howe (right) and Bobby Hull gave legitimacy to the upstart WHA.

The first mention of the World Hockey Association in The Hockey News is in a Nov. 19, 1971 issue on page 3: 'New World Hockey League Eyeing October '72 Start With 10 Franchises Set.' The story is below the fold.

Above the fold is an NHL story that is clearly reaction to the WHA rumblings. 'Long Island, Atlanta Swell NHL To 16 Teams.' No way any WHA news was going to trump NHL headlines. The rivalry between the two leagues was akin to Hatfield vs. McCoy from Day 1.

"They tried to crush us from the get-go," said WHA co-founder Gary Davidson. "They sued us in every city they had a franchise and we had a franchise – and we countersued for anti-trust and won."

Davidson was a Santa Ana, Calif. lawyer who helped spearhead the formation of the American Basketball Association as a rival league to the NBA in 1967. When promoter Dennis Murphy approached him four years later with a far-fetched idea he had, the attorney jumped on it.

"Dennis came to me and said 'You know Gary, there's only one league in hockey,' and I said 'Oh, let's start another one,' " Davidson recalled.

"And I had never seen a hockey game at that time. Three guys from Canada came down to meet with us (Bill Hunter, Ben Hatskin and John Bassett). The next thing you know the NHL was trying to shut us down."

Neither Davidson nor Murphy had any hockey experience, which prompted a lot of NHL people to slough it off as a rouse. But the WHA didn't hesitate battling the NHL head to head, naming New York, Boston, Toronto and Chicago as locations for its 12-team launch in 1972.

The upstart league started operating as though it controlled the landscape with little regard for the NHL. It held a player draft in February and two weeks later goalie Bernie Parent from the Toronto Maple Leafs was the first player to announce he'd be playing in the WHA the next fall. That opened the floodgate for others. Before long, established NHLers such as Bobby Hull, Derek Sanderson, Ted Green and J-C Tremblay were announcing new lucrative deals in the fledgling league.

"Many in our league, including (NHL president) Clarence Campbell, said it would fold before it even started," said Philadelphia Flyers founder Ed Snider. "But I was worried because in studying the (American Basketball Association), the (American Football League) and other rival leagues, they may move cities, but what they do is start. I made a point of signing all our players and not lose anybody to the WHA. In fact, that helped us win the Stanley Cup (in 1974 and '75)."

"They tried to crush us from the get-go."
- Gary Davidson

The court battles began. That only intensified the rivalry. But the courts ruled in favor of the WHA and deemed the NHL's reserve clause to be not binding. WHA teams were offering better contracts and a lot of players bolted. Before the end of that first WHA season, Snider and New York Rangers president Bill Jennings hammered out a deal with WHA representatives that would have seen the NHL swallow 11 of the WHA's 12 teams for an expansion fee of $4 million apiece.

"That story was never reported," Snider said in 2010. "That never made it to the media. It was all set to happen. We could put those 11 teams in any city we wanted, but (Chicago owner) Bill Wirtz and Clarence Campbell led a group to censor us for even talking to them. They shot it down."

Howard Baldwin, founder of the WHA's New England Whalers, remembers that near resolution.

"That would have ended the rivalry right then, after the first season," Baldwin said. "That was the great untold story. A few people in the NHL got it, they realized if they could nip in the bud quickly, they should. Ed Snider and Bill Jennings, they got it early on. Ed was right on. Ed had the vision with Bill – hey we can get rid of this now and take in 11 teams. But Campbell wasn't for it.

"We duked it out, then by the end of the fourth year we looked at possible ways to put the leagues together."

Through the 1970s, WHA franchises were constantly on the move. Teams and the league struggled with financial instability, but NHL players still came and went. The WHA also provided an opportunity for NHL minor leaguers to play on the big stage, albeit in a rival league.

"There were a lot of veteran guys like myself who were on the fringe in the NHL, but wanted to take this chance," said Jack Stanfield, a 30-year-old career minor leaguer in 1972 who joined the Houston Aeros and later became the team's vice-president. "The NHL didn't like this either because it robbed their farm teams as well. I think it pissed them off. It was a thorn in their side."

The NHL kept expanding as well, adding Atlanta and the New York Islanders in 1972, and Washington and Kansas City in 1974 to get to 18 teams. But the WHA was more experimental. It realized there was a plethora of talent in Europe and the Winnipeg Jets hit the jackpot with the likes of Anders Hedberg and Ulf Nilsson. Overtime was a WHA creation.

"The quality of hockey was pretty good as well," said WHA historian Timothy Gassen. "(The NHL) lost every court case again the WHA and as part of the court settlement were forced to play pre-season games against the WHA. For five years, NHL playoff teams played WHA teams and in 80 games, the WHA won 45 of them. That's fascinating."

Not only did the WHA lure proven players away from the NHL, it also started taking building blocks in the form of yet-to-be-drafted teenagers in the late 1970s.

"When the really young players started to move, that's when you could tell things were going to get nasty," Stanfield said. "Take Mark and Marty Howe, Terry Ruskowski, Morris Lukowich, John Tonelli, the Baby

Bulls of Birmingham. Tonelli was only 18. Then Wayne Gretzky. I think it was the weight of all those young players moving that led to a resolution."

Michel Goulet was one of eight Baby Bulls in Birmingham in 1978-79. Other Bulls teenagers were Rick Vaive, Craig Hartsburg, Rob Ramage, Louis Sleigher, Gaston Gingras, Pat Riggin and Keith Crowder.

> **"When the really young players started to move, that's when you could tell things were going to get nasty."**
> **- Jack Stanfield**

"I scored 72 goals in 73 games at 17 (in the Quebec League)," Goulet recalled. "Mr. Gilles Leger (Birmingham GM) gave me a call and said they wanted to sign some underage players. I said, 'I'm interested.' I was making $16 a week, I can make $50,000 the first year, no problem. But you know what? It was not the money. It was, 'I think I can play.' "

The WHA was doing a great job getting under the skin of NHL owners and GMs, but it was the accountants who came to the NHL's rescue. Many WHA franchises were struggling financially and when a viable "absorption" proposal was tabled in 1979, the rival league's strongest teams – Edmonton Oilers, Winnipeg Jets, New England Whalers, Quebec Nordiques – figured the best chance to survive was to cross the line and become part of the NHL.

"Merger discussions failed three times," Baldwin said. "The fourth time we got the job done. Look, the NHL is a great league, they were smart. Who's kidding who, when we finally did the merger or expansion, we (the WHA) were suffering, but both leagues were suffering. They just had more troops."

Chicago Blackhawks owner Bill Wirtz was defiant as ever when the discussion of merger or absorption with the WHA came up. He put the muzzle on Snider in 1971-72 when the notion was proposed and even fought it in 1979 when it became inevitable, saying the WHA "cost the NHL $1 billion in lost revenue, we're not going to reward them."

Players, coaches, scouts and managers joined NHL teams and the hard feelings eventually evaporated. Thirty years later, many in the industry believe the WHA made for a healthier environment in pro hockey today.

"It totally changed the way we had to do business," Snider said.

"It made players realize there is money to be made out there," Stanfield said. "The big bonuses and salaries didn't go away when the WHA went under. NHLers started making better wages immediately."

"It opened up the game in the NHL in the 1980s," Baldwin said. "Take a look at the top 20 scorers the year after the WHA and NHL (merged.) You'll see at least five or six of them were WHA players."

BOSTON COLLEGE
BOSTON UNIVERSITY

VS.

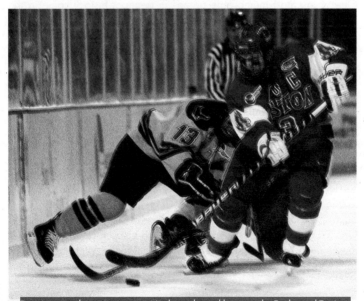

Even in an outdoor winter game, it's always heated between the Eagles and Terriers.

When it comes to rivalries in college sports, there is none bigger than the one between Boston College and Boston University.

The series began on Feb. 6, 1918, when the BC Eagles defeated the BU Terriers by a score of 3-1. More than 90 years later, the rivalry burns brighter than ever.

> **"He hit him right in the shins and under that costume the guy had to be in pain, it was pretty hard slash."**
> **- Rob Scuderi**

As of Mar. 1, 2010, the two teams have faced off 250 times, with the Terriers holding a 125-108-17 edge over the Eagles.

As far as games with meaning go, BU has won 29 of the 58 Beanpot tournaments, an annual meet between the four major college hockey schools in the Boston area. BC ranks second, winning the tournament 15 times. In total, BU has faced BC 20 times in the Beanpot final, with the Terriers coming out victorious 12 times.

One of the most memorable games in Beanpot history came in the 2000-01 final, when BC defeated BU 5-3. It was the first time BC had triumphed over BU in a Beanpot final in 25 years, having gone 0-7 against them during that span. Montreal Canadiens right winger Brian Gionta was captain of that Eagles team.

"It was my senior year and in my first three years our team had been to two NCAA finals, but everyone still judged us by our lack of Beanpot success," Gionta said. "To finally get over that hump and win the Beanpot on our way to a national championship was a huge thrill."

While BC has more Hockey East crowns with eight (BU has seven), the Terriers outshine the Eagles in national championships by a count of five to three.

On Jan. 8, 2010, the rivalry was made into a spectacle, becoming the third NCAA game in history to be played outdoors. With 40,000-plus fans cheering the teams on, BU edged BC 3-2 at a perfect setting for one of hockey's greatest rivalries, historic Fenway Park.

The two men who are most entrenched in the rivalry are Jack Parker and Jerry York, who are the legendary coaches of BU and BC, respectively.

Parker has coached the Terriers since 1973, while York has led the Eagles since 1994. Both men are graduates of their respective schools and were on-ice rivals from 1965 to 1967.

"They are the epitome of rivalries in college sports as far as coaches go," said L.A.'s Rob Scuderi, whose 168 games played for BC is the most in the team's history, a number he shares with Mike Brennan.

But for two men who spent the past 16 years battling in the BC vs. BU war, they leave the rivalry on the ice.

"They're actually pretty good friends off the ice," said Brandon Yip, who tallied the game-winner against BC in the 2006 Hockey East Championship. "They play tennis a lot and communicate with each other all the time. Once the game starts, though, they become enemies. They've played countless games against each other, but I'm sure every time they face off its special for them."

Though the rivalry may have started on the ice, it's gone way beyond that. BU/BC games are always played in front of a packed house, with the fans getting just as into the rivalry as the players do. Sometimes, even the mascots get involved.

"I remember one time one of our guys took a pretty good slash at the BU mascot, which is a big, stupid terrier," Scuderi recalled. "He hit him right in the shins and under that costume the guy had to be a pain, it was pretty hard slash."

Now a member of the NHL's Colorado Avalanche, Yip has gotten his feet wet in a few big rivalries at hockey's highest level, but says nothing compares to the one he was part of during his college years.

"Coming into Colorado and playing teams like Detroit and Calgary, those are huge games for us," Yip said. "Coming from Boston, I guess I'm a little prejudiced, but nothing beats the BU/BC rivalry."

VS.

CHICOUTIMI SAGUENEENS
QUEBEC REMPARTS

Richard Martel has been coaching in the Quebec League for the past 20 seasons.

"I've been part of many great rivalries in this league, but Chicoutimi-Quebec is the biggest one by far," said the Chicoutimi Saguenéens bench boss. "The two cities are less than two hours apart and there's so much media coverage when we play each other.

"There's always extra spark and electricity in the building when it's Chicoutimi versus Quebec. It's a game like no other whenever these two clubs meet. I know for our fans that Quebec is the team they want to see us beat the most."

> **"All eyes in Quebec were focused on that series and both buildings were sold out for every game."**
> **- Richard Martel**

Martel still refuses to discuss an ugly incident that happened in Game 2 of a first round playoff series on March 22, 2008. With the Quebec Remparts facing a six-goal deficit, a 10-player brawl broke loose and developed into even more of a circus when the goaltenders got involved.

Quebec goaltender Jonathan Roy skated the length of the ice and delivered a pounding on Chicoutimi's Bobby Nadeau, who didn't fight back. Roy then gave the crowd in the packed Chicoutimi stadium the finger with both hands as he left the ice.

The QMJHL suspended six players and two coaches for a total of 28 games and fined both clubs $4,000. The league was widely criticized for not coming down with stiff enough punishment.

"There's one thing I remember about that series," Martel said. "All games were televised around the province as if it was the league final. All eyes in Quebec were focused on that series and both buildings were sold out for every game. The fallout of that incident changed a lot of things in our league. There's tougher rules and less fights since then."

Quebec coach Patrick Roy was handed a five-game suspension for his "prejudicial conduct." He was caught on camera gesturing to his son Jonathan before he went after the opposition goaltender, but he denied encouraging the fight.

The elder Roy, an NHL Hall of Famer, apologized and admitted that if he had better controlled the situation, his son wouldn't have ended up at the center of a controversy.

Quebec-Chicoutimi is a natural rivalry that doesn't require any marketing gimmicks. There's been a long-standing bitter feud between these clubs, but that's especially true since their infamous playoff game, which drew national media coverage.

Television stations across the country showed video of that line brawl countless times. People flocked to YouTube and watched in disbelief as things deteriorated to the point of being out of control.

"First, these cities aren't far apart," said Roy, a four-time Stanley Cup winner. "Second, we've played each other a lot in the playoffs and I think that does have an effect. I also think the media has played a role in this rivalry.

"When Chicoutimi comes to town, it's the game that's the easiest to sell to our fans. Our players are talking about these games more. No matter where these two teams are in the standings, it's always hard-fought games between us. I think a rivalry like this is great for the league."

Quebec Education and Sports Minister Michelle Courchesne met with QMJHL commissioner Gilles Courteau in the aftermath of the controversial Quebec-Chicoutimi playoff game. They worked together to introduce new measures aimed at stopping needless violence in amateur hockey in Quebec.

The QMJHL knew that it needed to get tougher with its punishment following that black mark. The league had to police itself with more authority or risk having Quebec's provincial government enter with an iron fist.

There have been lots of great QMJHL rivalries over the years, but none have had as much impact on the league as Quebec-Chicoutimi. This is a battle that ultimately impacted all 18 teams because it led to changing league disciplinary procedures.

> **"When we arrived in Chicoutimi the police were there waiting for us."**
> **- Kelsey Tessier**

Quebec center Kelsey Tessier experienced the rivalry against Chicoutimi for three-and-a-half seasons. He noted that it turns into an intense playoff atmosphere every time these clubs meet, even if it's just a pre-season game.

"Even if one team is better than the other, it doesn't matter," he said. "It's always hard-fought games between these teams. It's a great show. The crowds make it more exciting in both buildings because there's lots of fans who travel to watch their team on the road.

"In Quebec, there's always 15,000 fans for these games and it's sold out two weeks in advance. Chicoutimi brings five fan buses when they come and it's all blue and red (the two teams' colors) in the crowd. I think every junior hockey fan should come to one of these games just to experience it."

Quebec went on to win 4-2 in that infamous playoff series against Chicoutimi. It was well-controlled after the Game 2 blowup.

"After that game, there was extra security for the teams in both rinks," Tessier recalled. "When we arrived in Chicoutimi the police were there waiting for us. They had to escort our team bus into the city. That's something I will always remember. It was really intense.

"It was pretty weird because the two teams did separate warmups for the rest of that series. When we went to Chicoutimi they didn't even play music for our warmup. When they came into our rink we put classical music on for their warmup. It was a lot of fun and games."

Nicolas Deschamps, a left winger and Anaheim Ducks draft pick, played two and a half seasons for Chicoutimi.

"It's always a war against Quebec," he said. "There was so much animosity between the clubs. It was fun to play those games. Both buildings are full and the fans are really into it. After each whistle, there's a scrum.

"Those games were different than any other we played just because of the emotion and bad feelings between the clubs. You have those games circled on the calendar. It felt like a playoff game every time we played them."

PETER KARMANOS
MIKE ILITCH

VS.

It all started with 12-year-olds, between midgets, peewees, bantams and squirts. Before too long, Michael Ilitch and Peter Karmanos Jr. were fighting over the Stanley Cup itself.

Detroit and Carolina may not be natural rivals, but their respective owners have gone at it before.

The rivalry between Ilitch, the Detroit pizza baron and owner of the Red Wings, and Karmanos, the Detroit software magnate and owner of the Carolina Hurricanes, is one of the oddest – and fiercest – in sports.

"I have no use for Mike Ilitch." – Peter Karmanos

Their personal enmity has seen teams evicted from arenas and players offered millions of dollars – with the Cup hanging in the balance. The 2002 Cup final saw the millionaires' private spat writ large across the face of hockey when the elite Red Wings and upstart Hurricanes brought the two feuding owners to the forefront.

"If there's acrimony – if – we share it equally," Karmanos dead-panned before Game 1. Six months earlier, in an interview in his office, his tone was a little different: "I have no use for Mike Ilitch."

The rivalry between the two has its roots in minor hockey in the 1970s, when Karmanos started Compuware's youth operation to compete with Ilitch's established Little Caesar's program. The fact that Karmanos is the son of Greek immigrants and Ilitch the son of Macedonian immigrants, who grew up in Detroit neighborhoods that didn't see eye-to-eye either, may play into it as well.

Since then, the two have fought it out at every level of hockey. Relations between the Detroit titans reached a nadir in 1995, when Ilitch declined to renew Karmanos' lease at Joe Louis Arena for his Ontario League Junior Red Wings. Ilitch's public justification was that the building was better served hosting concerts than junior hockey, but Karmanos – a longtime Red Wings season-ticket holder – had openly rooted for the New Jersey Devils to beat the Red Wings that spring.

Three years later, Karmanos took his revenge. Red Wings star Sergei Fedorov was in the middle of a contract dispute when Karmanos stepped in with an offer sheet. Karmanos' public justification was that a star like Fedorov was exactly what the fledgling Hurricanes needed to take root in North Carolina, but the offer was loaded with huge bonus payments that would only have to be made if Fedorov reached the conference final.

The struggling Hurricanes were unlikely to make it that far. The Red Wings did – and ended up paying Fedorov a $12 million bonus after matching Carolina's offer. All told, Karmanos' offer sheet cost Ilitch $26 million in bonuses.

Time has passed, and the relationship has thawed somewhat of late. In March, Karmanos' Plymouth Whalers – direct descendents of the Jr. Red Wings – became the latest Detroit-area OHL team to enjoy a practice day at Joe Louis as guests of the NHL Red Wings, their first appearance there since getting the boot.

Off the ice, Karmanos and Ilitch are both major contributors to a public-private partnership that is funding a light-rail project on Detroit's Woodward Avenue, helping to raise $125 million. It's the latest in an increasingly long list of occasions where Karmanos and Ilitch have joined forces in support of the revitalization of downtown Detroit.

Nevertheless, there's always something extra on the line when the Hurricanes and Red Wings face off, whether on the game's biggest stage or in a September rookie camp scrimmage – or, for that matter, whenever rival 12-year-olds take up the banner.

> "If there's acrimony...we share it equally."
> – Peter Karmanos

VS. RUSS CONWAY
ALAN EAGLESON

Bobby Orr was the man who introduced Alan Eagleson to Russ Conway. An unwitting and unfortunate victim of hockey's greatest-ever scam artist, Orr at least can take solace in the fact he made the initial connection between hockey's most powerful man and the journalist who helped bring him down.

Eagleson was the founding executive director of the NHL Players' Association and the promoter behind the 1972 Summit Series. He was also the player agent for Orr and many other players during the league's heydays of the 1970s. He was the self-proclaimed hockey czar.

Conway was sports editor for the *Eagle-Tribune*, a small newspaper based out of Lawrence, Mass. He started covering Boston Bruins games in the 1960s and the publication had a well-earned reputation for quality journalism. Conway kept in touch with Eagleson through the 1970s, saying he was a good source for big stories such as the 1976 Canada Cup and the NHL merger with the World Hockey Association.

"I could call him at home, call him direct at the office," Conway said. "We were pretty close for a lot of years."

"We were pretty close for a lot of years."
- Russ Conway

But during that time, Conway also heard grumbling from players unhappy with Eagleson's leadership. He kept those notes – and those connections. By 1989, growing unrest among player agents and accusations of misdirection and misappropriation of union funds prompted Eagleson to announce he'd be retiring from the NHLPA position in 1992.

By June, 1991, Conway had accumulated enough evidence to go forth with a series of articles in the *Eagle-Tribune* exposing Eagleson for the scoundrel a U.S. grand jury eventually determined he was. Eagleson was eventually charged with fraud, theft, racketeering, obstruction of justice and embezzlement, and sentenced in 1998 to 18 months in prison.

> **"His only response to one question I had was asking me, 'Have you stopped beating your wife?' "**
> **– Bruce Dowbiggin**

Conway said he first confronted Eagleson about the allegations in July, 1991. After a quick round of niceties, Conway told the union head what the *Eagle-Tribune* was about to run. That was met with a barrage of cursing.

"The last time I spoke with him was that infamous phone call," said Conway, now semi-retired and living part time in Pompano Beach, Fla. "He said, 'Good luck to you. Other people have tried. No one has gotten anywhere.' He hasn't talked to me in almost 20 years since. We exchanged glances in the courtroom, but that's it."

So call it a rivalry carried out in newsprint and courtrooms. Since that conversation, Conway said he has more than 25 documented interview requests that were rebuffed. In addition to the *Eagle-Tribune* articles, Conway wrote the book *Game Misconduct: Alan Eagleson and the Corruption of Hockey* in 1995. Conway was runner-up for the Pulitzer Prize in 1992.

During that period, CBC reporter Bruce Dowbiggin was researching and reporting the Eagleson saga from Canadian soil. Dowbiggin said the rivalry between Conway and Eagleson was one based strictly on duty and profession.

"I don't think it ever got personal between the two," Dowbiggin said. "Russ was a meticulous and factual reporter who documented every note, every phone call and Eagleson was just defending himself. I don't think they personalized it."

Even when Dowbiggin was chasing Eagleson with questions, Eagleson would dodge them like a street fighter. "His only response to one question I had was asking me, 'Have you stopped beating your wife?' " Dowbiggin said.

"Al's a weird dude. I'm on my way to court with him once because he's suing me for libel. His mother-in-law has just passed away a day or two before. I get on an elevator and there he is with the rest of the family. Out of respect I said, 'I'm sorry to hear about your mother-in-law.' Well, he starts telling a series of stories about her and the family and we're chatting like we're old friends rather than adversaries."

VS.

KEN HITCHCOCK
PUNCH MCLEAN

At the other end of the phone line is Ernie 'Punch' McLean, all larger-than-life 78 years old of him. He explains he hasn't been around much lately. He was just up in the Yukon staking gold claims and soon he's off to California to purchase more mining equipment.

No sooner does McLean hear the name Ken Hitchcock than he breaks out into a full-on belly laugh. Those were rollicking good times in the rough-and-tumble Western League, times when you could get away with a lot more stuff than you can now.

For the record, Hitchcock and McLean coached against each other only one season, the 1986-87 campaign when Hitchcock led the powerhouse Kamloops Blazers and McLean was behind the bench for the hapless New Westminster Bruins.

But McLean was always around the Bruins, the first incarnation of which he led to four Western League championships and two Memorial Cups, and the second one in which they played five rather non-descript years before morphing into the Tri-City Americans. The Bruins and Blazers were heated rivals and the battles between Hitchcock and McLean were legendary.

> **"You think your team is tough? Try playing in New West and have fun."**
> **- Ken Hitchcock**

One time during that season, right in the middle of a game, McLean waved a hot dog at Hitchcock on the Kamloops bench. Hitchcock responded by covering up his left eye.

Doesn't sound terribly outlandish, does it? Not until you consider that, at the time, Hitchcock was morbidly obese and well on his way to becoming a 450-pounder. Or until you consider that 15 years prior to that, McLean lost his left eye when he crashed his plane into a clump of trees in Saskatchewan. McLean would later joke that he somehow managed to crash into the only tree on the prairies.

Before coming to the NHL, Ken Hitchcock matched wits with legendary junior coach Punch McLean in the Western League.

"I don't know what made me do it," Hitchcock recalled. "He was ridiculing me and I thought I had to get him back and that was the only thing that came to my mind. I don't think Ernie thought I would do what I did and I think he thought it was pretty funny."

The battles between the Blazers and Bruins were very real and very intense. The rivalry between the two men who coached the teams was also real. But as is often the case in major junior hockey, it had as much to do with creating a buzz as it did hard feelings and competition. McLean is a veteran of the business side of junior hockey and he realized that people come to watch good teams, really tough players and rivals who had the ability to lay it on thick in the name of promoting the next game.

"You can't do things like that now," McLean said. "In junior hockey, if there were no asses in the seats, you didn't make any money. So you were always doing something different."

Like sending 10 pizzas to the visitors' bench of the Queen's Park Arena when the Blazers were in town?

"Yeah, stuff like that," McLean said. "I had to admit, I did that."

"The guy came to our bench and he had one of those great big white hats on," Hitchcock said. "What could we do? We kept them. We put them in our dressing room and we had them after the game."

"They didn't trade for Mark Recchi...they stole him." - Punch McLean

In fact, after the hot dog/eye-covering incident, the two teams capitalized on it. For the next game between the Blazers and Bruins in Kamloops, the team had an "Eye Patch Night" promotion in which McLean cooperated.

"He was really good about it," Hitchcock said. "He was really into it and he made it a fun event for everybody."

The Blazers, who ironically were created out of the ashes of the first New Westminster Bruins franchise, got the better of the Bruins on and off the ice for the most part. The Blazers were always a championship contender and managed to trade for a young Mark Recchi from the Bruins in 1986 when McLean was out looking for gold in the off-season. The move did not go over well with McLean and Hitchcock claims there was no shortage of derision shown to him because of the deal.

"They didn't trade for Mark Recchi," McLean said, "they stole him. Hitch gave me three guys who couldn't play, couldn't skate, couldn't shoot."

They were able to shoot well enough to score a couple of goals against the Blazers in their first game between the two teams, though. "I remember after they scored, they threw the pucks into our bench."

Part of the dynamic was that Hitchcock was a young, unproven coach in the league and McLean was a coaching legend in the WHL. McLean said there were times when he would approach Hitchcock to talk before a game, only to have Hitchcock retreat to the dressing room.

"I think he thought I was playing head games with him," McLean said.

Hitchcock admitted that he was intimidated by coaching against a junior hockey legend.

"I was afraid of him," Hitchcock said. "You think your team is tough? Try playing in New West and have fun. There was a price to pay to win in New West and you'd better be prepared to pay it."

Hitchcock and McLean are now great friends and enjoy reminiscing about their junior hockey games when they meet. McLean is a fixture at Vancouver Canucks games and was at GM Place for the Olympics when Hitchcock was with the Canadian team as an assistant coach.

As for McLean, he continues to make headlines. In August of 2009 while staking a claim in Dease Lake in northern B.C., McLean fell down a steep embankment. When he came to, he was disoriented and had lost his GPS equipment, his cell phone and his food. He wandered around the area for four days before being found by searchers.

"He has nine lives," Hitchcock said, "and I think he's on No. 14 already."

TSN

CBC

It's always been a hard-fought battle for hockey broadcasting supremacy between CBC and TSN, but the events that unfolded in June 2008 were enough to shock people across Canada.

When CBC's license to use Dolores Claman's "The Hockey Theme" as the theme song for *Hockey Night in Canada* expired after the 2008 Stanley Cup playoffs, CBC was expected to renew it again. But after years of a poor relationship with the composer's agent and disputes over the worth of the song, CBC Sports executive director Scott Moore announced on June 6 that a deal could not be reached and they would no longer hold the rights to the iconic song. It had been the opening theme for *Hockey Night in Canada* since 1968.

When Rick Brace, President, Revenue, Business Planning and Sports, CTV Inc. heard the news, he knew he had to act quickly.

"I read the morning paper and found out that Scott Moore had announced they were unable to come to terms with [Claman]," he said. "I walked into the CEO's office that morning and said, 'The song's available, and it's an iconic theme and it seems like a tragedy to just go into the abyss.'"

The CEO agreed with Brace who immediately contacted Claman's agent. He confirmed that the song was still available, but Claman would rather sell out the rights to it in its entirety.

This began a short volley of negotiations between TSN and Claman, and by the next day, a deal had been smoothed out. TSN would pay $3 million to buy the rights for the iconic tune.

"I was surprised that CTV/TSN a) paid the amount of money they did for it and b) wanted the song," Moore said. "To me the song was so associated with CBC and *Hockey Night in Canada* that it was a surprise that another brand would want it for their broadcast. It was like Pepsi buying Coke's jingles."

TSN started using the newly acquired song for its hockey broadcasts as well as French broadcasts on RDS while CBC announced a nationwide contest for Canadian composers to submit a new theme.

"I think how we've come out of it on the other end is what I would have expected, but it was a little hard to put into perspective at the time," Moore said. "At the time it was disappointing, but we have a new piece of music that people like, and *Hockey Night in Canada* is about hockey on Saturday nights and tradition – not a piece of music."

"It was like Pepsi buying Coke's jingles."
- Scott Moore

But Brace said that even though people may still associate the song with *Hockey Night in Canada*, TSN still did the right thing to acquire it.

"A number of Canadians were probably angry to see it change hands – it's like the second Canadian national anthem – but CBC made the decision to walk away from it," he said. "That positioned us as kind of the saviors.

"Instead of walking in and stealing the song, we saved it."

Hockey Night in Canada still has the famous logo, but competitor TSN now has the classic theme song.

VS. ED BELFOUR
MARTY TURCO

Ed Belfour is a Mopar man.

You can catch him driving a Porsche or Mercedes every now and then, but as a car guy, he stays pretty close to the Plymouth, Dodge and Chrysler brands.

That explains a lot about Belfour. He is loyal…and he expects loyalty in return.

And that was the crux of Belfour's rivalry with Marty Turco back in the early 2000s.

Belfour's contract with the Dallas Stars was expiring after the 2001-02 season and he fully expected the team to offer him an extension. After all, in five years with the franchise, he had won the 1999 Stanley Cup, took the Stars to the 2000 final and added a 1998 trip to the Western Conference final. In his short span, he set most of the Stars regular season and playoff records.

But there was one little problem. Turco was 27 and had posted two seasons of backup play where he had a 2.00 goals-against average. He was ready to take over, so the Stars had to either move Turco or let Belfour go.

> **"We were never what you would call close."**
> **- Marty Turco**

"Ed is as competitive a person as I have ever known and he was very protective of his position," said former Stars coach Ken Hitchcock, who ended up getting let go during the final phases of the battle between the two goalies. "It was very hard, because Marty was playing great and we were in a playoff race."

Turco finished with a .921 save percentage while Belfour came in at .895 that season, and the writing on the wall became clear.

"I was just the young guy who did what the coach told me and wanted to help the team any way I could," Turco said. "I respected Ed a heck of a lot for everything he did, but we were never what you would call close."

Ed Belfour was one of the best and didn't like any competition.

Stars center Mike Modano said it was a tough time for both goalies.

"Nobody here is ever going to say a bad word about Ed because of what he's done for us," Modano noted. "But it wasn't pretty. He wasn't happy and he let people know about it."

Belfour had incidents before in Dallas, getting arrested for a fight in a hotel in 2000 and leaving the team in a dispute with Hitchcock in 2001.

There were also incidents of breaking up a video player or television after he was pulled in games. So there was always the need to keep a cushion around Belfour and Turco understood that.

"I never tried to push things with him," Turco said. "I just tried to do my job and let him do his."

"It wasn't pretty."
- Mike Modano

Ironicallly, Turco's personality is the exact opposite of Belfour's and since the break-up in 2002, Turco has befriended his backup goalies – all the way from Ron Tugnutt to Mike Smith to a brief run with Alex Auld in 2009-10.

"He's such a good guy and a great teammate," Auld said. "When I was traded, one of the first voicemails I had on the cell phone was from him, welcoming me here and saying how much he looks forward to becoming a goaltending tandem."

Turco said that's the way he believes a team has to operate.

"Obviously, I was able to learn a lot from Ed Belfour, but we looked at things very differently," Turco said. "To him, I think he felt he had to focus just on himself. To me, the greatest part of athletic achievement is to be a part of a great team. Y'know, as I get older though, I see the purpose of how he did his job. When you're a goalie, you have to find your own place and there was nobody better at doing that than him."

OTTAWA
ALEXEI YASHIN

VS.

Any group of angry fans can boo a villain. But it takes a special kind of hate to file a lawsuit against your hockey-playing anti-hero and burn him in effigy.

Those are just some of the measures Ottawa Senators' boosters took in expressing their contempt of one-time local favorite Alexei Yashin.

At issue was – what else? – money. Many Senators fans viewed the gifted Russian as a greedy, lazy, me-first individual, devoid of principle. The Yashin camp, conversely, said his holdout during the 1999-2000 season was all about integrity.

Alexei Yashin's time in Ottawa was turbulent to say the least.

Whatever the case, when Yashin threatened to withhold his services for the third time in five years despite being under contract, and the Sens called his bluff, public sentiment was squarely in the team's corner.

"Everywhere you went around town that year people were talking about Yashin," said Jim Boone, president of the NHL Fans Association and an Ottawa resident. "It was as big a deal here as the lockout was league-wide. There was so much anger towards this guy."

That wasn't always the case. The first player ever selected in an entry draft by the Sens (second overall in 1992), Yashin mostly lived up to the buzz that surrounded his lofty draft status. While the team struggled year after year, Yashin grew and eventually blossomed into a post-season NHL all-star and a Hart Trophy runner-up in 1999. That same year, he finished tied with Jaromir Jagr for second in the goal-scoring race with 44, just three behind league leader Teemu Selanne.

> "There was so much anger towards this guy."
> – Jim Boone

The problem was his namesake, Alexandre Daigle, the club's first overall selection in the 1993 draft. More precisely, it's the monster that Daigle became, as created by the franchise and media, that soured the scenario.

Daigle was a golden boy, a charismatic teen from nearby Quebec who was supposed to be the next big thing. Forecasting a potential for conflict, Yashin agent Mark Gandler said he went to the Senators to renegotiate for the first time in order to protect his client's interests and was assured the two Alexes would be paid on par. This transpired before Daigle's landmark five-year, $12.5 million-deal was inked, the largest pact ever for a first-year player.

"I don't want to say anything derogatory about the people involved," Gandler said, "but when Daigle's contract showed up, it was a 180 degree turnaround. We felt Alexei was slighted."

As the seasons passed and it became clear Yashin was the superior player, bad blood simmered and the Yashin camp went back to the trough a couple times looking to make good on what it says it was promised. The problem was, by the time the third occasion arose, the Sens had gone through a chorus line of GMs that included Mel Bridgman, Randy Sexton, Pierre Gauthier, Rick Dudley, and, finally, in 1999-2000, Marshall Johnston. Continuity was an issue, as were lack of funds for owner Rod Bryden, and Johnston says he wasn't made aware of any verbal agreements. What he knew categorically was Yashin was due $3.6 million in the final year of his deal and Johnston was going to draw a firm line. Play in Ottawa or play nowhere. No new pact, no trade out of town.

"I didn't know anything about the first two (renegotiations), it was before I got there," Johnston said. "I'm old-school in that you sign the contract, you live with the contract and then you move on to the next one. You don't try half-way through the contract and say, 'Oh, well, I didn't get enough' or 'they low-balled me.' "

The spat become very bitter and very public. The Sens spiked the propaganda war by releasing to the media a letter written to them by Gandler in which he stated their hard-line position. Yashin validated that it wasn't just the agent pulling strings when he told a reporter in the fall of 1999, "I can sit out two years if I have to." Owner Bryden's comeback? "Alexei Yashin? That name doesn't even register with me."

Further fueling hard feelings was the way the Sens had been stunned in the 1999 playoffs, being swept 4-0 in the first round by the underdog Sabres. Ottawa had finished second overall with 103 points, 12 more than Buffalo and, as the No. 2 seed, was supposed to roll over No. 7. Captain Yashin, expected to lead the charge, failed to register a point. Sens supporters were incredulous.

Not everyone agreed, however, the finger of blame should be pointed at Yashin.

"He had 24 shots on goal in four games," Dudley recalled. "We happened to play against Dominik Hasek. If anyone else was in goal, 'Yash' would have had four or five goals at least in those games. He played hard and he wanted it and it would be very difficult for someone to tell me anything different."

Still, the local critics became more vocal. They looked at his less-than-efficient skating style and accused him of apathy.

Yashin's image also took a severe pounding over a donation he'd made, then rescinded, to Ottawa's National Arts Centre in 1998. Yashin pledged $1 million to the hall over five years on a proviso; what that stipulation was depends on who you believe. Media reports said he demanded his parents be put on the payroll for $425,000 for consulting fees. Gandler says the figure was $60,000 for his mother only and was for legitimate services rendered: to secure high-level Russian performers, a task she was never allowed to complete.

"Alexei fulfilled the first year of the pledge," Gandler said, "(but) nobody from Russia was invited to perform. We met with the conductor and people from the Arts Centre and there was no plans to invite the Russians. They reneged on their promise and we feel that moral obligation was no longer there. Alexei had the right to pull the plug and he did."

More than anything, though, it was the decision to sit out an entire year that earned Yashin epic scorn. Things came to a head when an arbitrator ruled after the 1999-2000 campaign ended that Yashin – who'd spent much of the season practising with a team in Switzerland – still had to honor the final year of his contract before being granted free agency. He returned to Ottawa that autumn convinced he'd made the right decision and unwilling to show contrition. At his first media conference following his return to the Sens, he remained quietly defiant.

> ## "Alexei Yashin? That name doesn't even register with me."
> ## – Rod Bryden

"The media expected Alexei to say, 'I'm sorry, I made a mistake. I love my teammates, I love this town.' But Alexei said it how it was," Gandler recalled. "He was there because the arbitrator compelled him to play. Otherwise, he wouldn't have gone back."

It was a dreadful experience for the Russian, who was mercilessly booed by the hometown fans much of the season. One irate zealot launched a $27.5-million lawsuit against him, claiming breach of contract. It was eventually tossed out of court. Others burned him in effigy.

"We knew that he was going to be under fire," Gandler said. "I can tell you, to play all year under those circumstances when your own fans boo you when you touch the puck – and score 40 goals – that's not easy. You have to be made of iron. He went through a tough time, no question about it."

Paradoxically, while the fans were taking out their anger, those in the organization have only fond memories of Yashin the person and player.

"I enjoyed 'Yash,' " Dudley said. "I thought he was a good guy and a good person and I thought he played hard for us."

Says Johnston: "I have nothing negative to say about him. He was a good guy. He wasn't any problems off the ice. He was a durable player. He was a good player."

And captain Daniel Alfredsson: "He was a quiet person, but he was good as a teammate. He cared about his teammates, no question."

There was a silver lining to the affair – maybe a couple. Johnston traded Yashin to the Islanders for Zdeno Chara, Bill Muckalt and New York's second overall pick, which Ottawa spent on Jason Spezza. As for Yashin, he finally scored that mega-deal, one-upping Daigle and then some when he accepted an $87.5-million payout over 10 years from the generous Isles.

And to this day both camps remain steadfast in the approaches they took. "I'm glad it turned out the way it did," Johnston says. "I know I wouldn't have done anything differently."

Said Gandler: "Had we known the result in advance, we'd do it again. No matter what."

HAROLD BALLARD

TORONTO

Though his name is infamous in Toronto, Harold Ballard is often referred to with bemusement by his former employees, even the ones he would mercilessly trash in order to get in the headlines.

Owner of the Maple Leafs from 1972 until his death in 1990, Ballard had first bought into the operation as a part-owner in 1962, along with Stafford Smythe and John Bassett Sr.

But once Ballard and his idiosyncratic ways took hold full-time, the Maple Leafs fell into a state of ruin until he passed away. Under his reign, the 'Buds' never won a division title, never appeared in the Stanley Cup final and rarely had any semblance of continuity.

Ballard went through 11 coaching changes in 18 years, once firing the legendary Roger Neilson, then offering him his job back if he wore a paper bag over his head. Neilson only accepted the former.

The fact Ballard made his affairs so public was part of his hubris, but also an integral part of his personality. He would be very cordial to players and staff to their faces, then turn around and rip them publicly in the press.

"He was the opposite of most bosses today," said Gord Stellick, who was GM of the team for just one season (1988-89), but was part of the organization since his youth. "He knew that to get Page 1, you had to say something outrageous."

Bruce Boudreau, now known as the coach who turned around the Washington Capitals, was Maple Leafs property during the Ballard era and played 134 games in the NHL for Toronto between stops in the minors. He remembered a very nice owner, though he did so cautiously.

"He always said hi, he always smiling," Boudreau recalled. "To my face, he was great."

And therein was the rub.

> **"We couldn't bring in the top hockey people, because he wouldn't pay them and they wouldn't want to work for him."**
> **- Rick Vaive**

Stellick recalled one incident on a team flight when, ravaged by injuries, the Leafs had called upon Czechoslovakian import Miroslav Ihnacak to step in. Ballard, a virulent anti-communist, had helped bring Ihnacak over to North America and freedom from Soviet rule, but felt he had been sold a bill of goods when the import failed to put up numbers at the NHL level.

As Ihnacak walked down the aisle to get to his seat, Ballard heartily welcomed him onto the flight. Ihnacak responded in kind, thanking Ballard for the opportunity before proceeding down the aisle.

"As he walked away," Stellick recalled, "Ballard turned to me and said 'boy, we're really scraping the bottom of the barrel now, aren't we?' "

Another infamous incident occurred after a member of the press noted to Ballard that star right winger Rick Vaive was up for another contract. Vaive had led the team in scoring two of the past three seasons.

"He told him 'Vaive would be a mediocre player in a six-team league, I'm not paying him another dime,' " Vaive said. "It didn't bother me – I (eventually) got a raise. It was after my third 50-goal season."

But that sense of entitlement was always the death of Ballard. He was the owner and he treated the organization as such. It was his way or the highway and unfortunately, the man didn't know how to win NHL hockey games.

"The building was his domain," Stellick said. "He signed the checks, he was front and center. He wanted to win, but he couldn't make the sacrifice of not meddling."

Added Vaive: "We had a lot of good hockey players, but we couldn't bring in the top hockey people, because he wouldn't pay them and they wouldn't want to work for him."

Ballard's legendary cheapness – which defenders point out was off-set by his many contributions to charity (which itself was off-set by the fact he was convicted of 47 counts of theft and fraud involving Maple Leafs money in 1972) – also damaged the ability of Maple Leafs players from putting in maximum effort.

Back in the 1980s, Ballard skirted NHL per diem rules by having flights take off five minutes after the cut-off of 7:30 p.m.

"It was only a half day he would have had to pay anyway," Vaive said. "There would be delays and they weren't jets back then, they were turbo-props. So we would get in to St. Louis or Minnesota at 11 p.m. or midnight. Eventually we sat down and said we would give up the meal money if we could just leave at a decent time, like 4:30 p.m., so we could get a good rest and go out for a meal. We did that for awhile."

Ironically, though, Vaive did admit to one benefit in flying commercial at the time.

"Because we would stay overnight instead of flying right home, guys started hanging out more and getting to know each other," he said. "I think it was beneficial to us."

But even when Ballard began to inch towards modernity, his scowling nature would pull him back to the dark side. The team eventually took charters, but it was a bumpy transition.

One night, a stewardess was coming down the aisle with little chocolate bars after dinner. King Clancy, Ballard's best friend and a longtime Leafs executive, told her that Ballard, sitting two rows behind, could only have one because he was diabetic.

"When she came to Ballard, he put his whole paw in, so she slapped his hand and told him 'you can only have one,' " Vaive noted. "He cancelled the charter, so we flew commercial the rest of the year."

Despite his crusty exterior, many of his former charges remember a softer side to Ballard. Stellick recalled a man who could pass for your favorite uncle when he was in a good mood, while Vaive thinks he has an idea of why Ballard was so sour in his final years.

"When King Clancy was alive, Harold was a different person," Vaive said. "After King passed, he became very grumpy, worse in his dislikes for things.

"That was his best friend, probably the only friend he had. You always hear about when a spouse dies after a long marriage, the other person goes downhill fast? It was very similar."

VS. NEW YORK RANGERS BOSTON BRUINS

Switching from one side of a bitter feud to the other in the prime of your career is a tough thing, especially when the hatred you have for the city you're now expected to represent has been clearly stated in book form.

Brad Park was 27 years old and Broadway to the bone when the New York Rangers traded him along with Jean Ratelle to the archrival Boston Bruins for Phil Esposito and Carol Vadnais in November of 1975.

A few years earlier, in his book *Play the Man*, Park spelled out in no uncertain terms how he felt about Boston and Bruins fans.

"He hated Boston," said Stan Fischler, a longtime hockey writer and broadcaster who ghostwrote Park's book.

And the feeling was mutual. Getting Bostonians angered by anything New York-related is no more difficult a task than finding a proud Texan, but B's supporters took their hostilities to another level when Park came to play their team.

"When I was with the Rangers, I was public enemy No. 1," Park said. "The FBI used to escort me on and off the ice in the Boston arena because of the hate mail I got."

That made it all the tougher for anybody in the game to wrap their head around the swap cooked up by Rangers GM Emile Francis and Bruins boss Harry Sinden.

The headline in The Hockey News read: 'Espo Crushed – Park Stunned As Shocked Hockey World Ponders Trade.'

The story, written by Norman MacLean in New York, described Esposito as a "hated ogre" at Madison Square Garden.

Ratelle was second on the Rangers' list of all-time scorers with 336 goals and 817 points in 862 games when the deal went down. A classy, reserved player, Ratelle couldn't hide his feelings on the move.

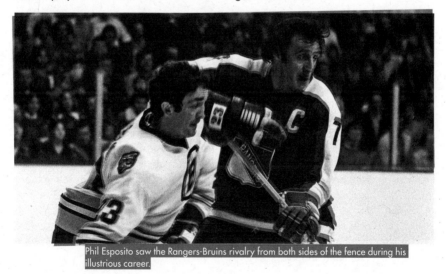

Phil Esposito saw the Rangers-Bruins rivalry from both sides of the fence during his illustrious career.

"I've been in New York 15 years and leaving the city will be a big problem for me," he told THN at the time.

One could be forgiven for thinking the bigger problem for Park was heading off to represent a city and team he'd previously required law enforcement protection from.

However, Park's competitive spirit ensured he'd put on the black and gold and do his best to prove the Blueshirts made a mistake.

"I'm going to show the Rangers that Boston got the better of the deal," he told THN. "Yes, I'm reporting, what else would I do, work in a mine?"

Thirty-five years later, Park admits that despite his conviction to come back and bite his old employer, he was – as always – going to keep his head up upon landing in Massachusetts.

> ## "The FBI used to escort me on and off the ice."
> ## – Brad Park

"I was looking over my shoulder," he said. "There was a point where we went on the road, and we lost the first game and we came back to Boston and we're winning like 6-0, got three power play goals, and some guy yells out, 'Hey Park, welcome to Boston.'

"Coming to Boston, once they saw how I was on the point, playing with Bobby Orr and how good the power play was going, they accepted it very quickly."

Perhaps more than any conflict in hockey, the New York-Boston hate is as much about the cities themselves as the teams that represent them. That explains why the rivalry still exists today, despite the fact the Bruins and Rangers haven't squared off in a playoff series since 1973. Bostonians relish any chance they get to take a bite out of Big Apple egos, while Fischler, a lifetime New Yorker, is only too happy to share the prevailing view in his city that Boston is a "two-bit town with a lousy subway."

He also enjoys sharing tales from the rivalry's earlier days, back when both clubs were struggling to keep up with the rest of the pack in the six-team league.

"The Rangers had a lot of trouble after World War II making the playoffs and for a stretch of several years they would always be beaten out for the fourth spot by the Bruins," said Fischler, who actually worked for the Rangers in 1954-55. "And they did it in a lot of dirty ways.

"I remember, one year for example, Milt Schmidt, he was a star center for the Bruins and the Rangers had a star center named Edgar Laprade. There was about a week-and-a-half left in the season and Schmidt broke Laprade's leg and that was the end of the Rangers."

Another sinister seed was sewn in those days when coach Lynn Patrick jumped ship from the Rangers to Boston in the summer of 1950. New York was coming off a stunning playoff run in which it upset the mighty Montreal Canadiens in the semifinal and took the powerhouse Detroit Red Wings to double overtime of Game 7 in the final before finally falling.

The fact the Rangers had come so close made Patrick's decision to bolt for a new bench all the harder to take – but all the easier to hate Boston. A few seasons later, Phil Watson was coaching the Rangers and Patrick delighted in verbally jabbing the man who held his old job when the hockey writers would gather with Watson – who, despite his English name, was actually French-Canadian – and the coach of the Rangers' next opponent every Tuesday at noon at a restaurant near MSG.

"The coach of the Bruins was Lynn Patrick; articulate, witty and in fact he'd been a teammate of Watson's (with the Rangers)," Fischler said. "Every session, when they would be in town, it was just hilarious to watch how Lynn Patrick would ridicule Watson and Watson, with no command of the language – he'd talk half in French and half in English and make no sense at all."

Rangers and Bruins fans, however, never seem to have trouble communicating very directly with each other and, according to Fischler, the heyday for strife between the cities was back in the black-and-blue 1970s.

"If you were a Ranger fan and you went to Boston Garden in those days, you took your life in your hands," he said. "And I speak first-hand."

> **"If you were a Ranger fan and you went to Boston Garden in those days, you took your life in your hands."**
> **– Stan Fischler**

VS. PATRICK ROY
MONTREAL CANADIENS

It was a defining moment in the histories of both the player and the franchise.

On Dec. 2 1995, the Montreal Canadiens were absorbing an offensive beating at the hands of the visiting Detroit Red Wings. Getting little help from his defense, superstar goalie Patrick Roy was having an off night and had surrendered seven goals just midway through the second period.

The home crowd was starting to razz Roy and he responded to their sarcastic cheers after a routine save by thrusting his arms in the air in mock celebration. After two more Detroit goals pushed the score to 9-1, coach Mario Tremblay finally pulled Roy from the game. It was still the second period.

Roy came to the bench, brushed past Tremblay without looking at him, then doubled back to confront team president Ronald Corey, who was sitting nearby in the stands. The legendary netminder told Corey he had just played his last game in Montreal. Days later, Roy was dealt to the Colorado Avalanche along with Mike Keane for Jocelyn Thibault, Andrei Kovalenko and Martin Rucinsky.

> **"I think as players, we all knew how much he wanted to win that game."**
> **- Mike Ricci**

While the Habs and Roy eventually mended fences, with the netminder's No. 33 being raised to the rafters of the Bell Centre in 2009, the rift at the time shifted the balance of power in the NHL.

With Roy in net, the Avs won their first Stanley Cup that spring, while the Canadiens haven't made a Cup final. Roy led Colorado back to the Cup in 2001, where he earned his third career Conn Smythe Trophy – the only player with that many – and fourth championship ring overall.

Roy did not want to revisit the episode, but several of his former teammates in Colorado recall just how intense the scene was when the fiery

Patrick Roy's final game as a Montreal Canadien was as controversial as they come.

goaltender squared off against his former Canadiens mates for the first time in Montreal after the trade.

"You could cut the tension with a knife," said Warren Rychel. "We had a large French contingent on the team, so it was huge and it was a great atmosphere."

Mike Ricci, who had himself been involved in a controversial trade when he was sent to Quebec in the Eric Lindros deal, remembered Roy's determination that night.

"I think as players, we all knew how much he wanted to win that game," Ricci recalled. "He never badmouthed Montreal, (but) we knew he wasn't very happy with the way everything went down…and he kinda walked up to the board, put some cash on the board and just looked at everybody and said, 'We win tonight.' I think we beat them 5-1 or 5-2 and that's when we became a team."

The irony of course, is that the Colorado Avalanche likely would have never acquired Roy if the franchise was still in its original setting as the Quebec Nordiques, Montreal's hated provincial rival.

"He respected us for going out and putting out a good effort," Ricci said. "And he realized that we were behind him and would do anything to help him get what we all wanted."

As intense a competitor as they come, the fact Roy's demands to leave Montreal were met had a lot to do with the confidence he had in himself and isn't necessarily a recommended negotiating strategy for every NHLer.

"If there was a guy who could get away with it, it was him," said Rychel, who still talks with Roy frequently. "Patrick is Patrick and that's the way he rolls."

VS. DON CHERRY
RON WILSON

If there is an ongoing feud between coaching legend Don Cherry and Toronto Maple Leafs coach Ron Wilson, it's easy to understand how it came about.

Sure, both men are similar in the relish with which they take on particular media members. And yes, both have had their share of successes behind the bench: Cherry won the NHL's Jack Adams award as its best coach in 1976; and Wilson has helmed Team USA to the championship of the 1996 World Cup of Hockey and has led NHL teams to more than 500 wins during his coaching career.

> **"I have no use for a guy who runs his players down to show how good a coach he is."**
> **- Don Cherry**

But as viewers of *Hockey Night in Canada* are well aware, Cherry is an avowed advocate of North American players who would sooner use his costume closet as the base of a massive polyester fire than live and play the game in Europe – the way Wilson did.

As well, Wilson is known as one of the NHL's more progressive-minded bench bosses, while Cherry's philosophy on most things is, to say the least, on the conservative side. So when Cherry chose to regularly tee off on Wilson once he became Leafs coach in 2008, few eyebrows were raised.

"When I am asked about him, I have no problem answering that I have no use for a guy who runs his players down to show how good a coach he is," Cherry told Toronto sports radio station The Fan 590 in 2009. "I think it's garbage."

From his *Coach's Corner* pulpit and in additional media interviews, Cherry also has referred to Wilson as, among other things, "Napoleon", "pompous and arrogant", "a typical American" (in spite of the fact Wilson was born in Windsor, Ont. and holds both Canadian and American citizenship) and "a bully."

So it is a feud – although as of early 2010 it seemed somewhat one-sided, given the scarcity of public comments from Wilson.

Ron Wilson quickly got under Don Cherry's skin when he became coach of the Toronto Maple Leafs.

"I'm just not going to comment on (Cherry's remarks)," Wilson said in a 2008 post-game press conference. "I think that irritates him more. He's entitled to his opinion…I have my style of coaching and I've been relatively successful at it and that's what I'm going to do."

An NHL GM who knows both men wasn't aware of a single incident that created the enmity between them; rather, he believes it was "different choices in their lives that led them where they are today."

"Ronnie was never and is never going to get into a war of words with Don," said the veteran GM. "You don't coach 1,000 games in this league without having some smarts, and Ron knows what a monumental battle it would be trying to win a war in the press with a Canadian icon.

> "I'm just not going to comment...
> I think that irritates him more."
> - Ron Wilson

"And he's a strong personality, just like Don is...I think that's probably the main driver of why the two of them wind up on opposite sides."

When asked whether he saw a scenario where amends between Wilson and Cherry could be made, the GM chuckled before answering.

"Yes — if there was a six-figure payoff involved," he said. "And that's to each of them."

SERGEI GONCHAR
WASHINGTON CAPITALS FANS

Sergei Gonchar may not have started this rivalry and he may not even be the last to take part in it, but he is the current placeholder for razzing at the Verizon Center in Washington.

An invaluable member of the Pittsburgh Penguins' 2009 Stanley Cup team, Gonchar isn't booed by rival Washington Capitals fans; for him they reserve a special 'Whooop!' chant that harkens back to the days the Caps faithful jeered former blueliner Larry Murphy.

Sergei Gonchar has been a target of Washington fans since leaving the Capitals.

Murphy's appointment to the Hall of Fame was based more on the strength of his excellent offensive skills and not his shutdown ability. Because of this, there were some shortcomings that Caps fans would remind him of, especially once he left Washington and joined the hated Penguins.

"When I got to Pittsburgh, it really started to take on a huge life," Murphy recalled. "I remember when I returned to Washington, the fans did that the first time I grabbed hold of the puck. When I got back to the bench, the guys were looking at me, going, 'What the hell was that?' " Mike Rucki, a longtime Capitals fan and blogger who covers Washington games for On Frozen Blog, can explain.

"Some believed it was *'wuss,'* but it was actually more like *'oops,* you weren't playing so well,' " Rucki noted. "It's gotta be reserved for an ex-Cap and one who had some issues when he was here. Jaromir Jagr got some when he came back with the New York Rangers – boy, he clearly did not want to come to D.C. – and I've heard Brendan Witt being 'whooped.' "

And those ground rules are entrenched.

"You wouldn't whoop Sidney Crosby, because he never played here," Rucki said. Similarly, even though Caps great Peter Bondra returned as a member of the Ottawa Senators, Atlanta Thrashers and Chicago Blackhawks, his was a Washington career held in the greatest esteem by the locals, while the hard-working Brian Pothier was dealt at the 2010 trade deadline without incident.

Which brings us back to Gonchar. A stalwart defenseman now, his penance is being paid for in part, but not exclusively, to a gaffe way back in 2001, when the Capitals were facing Pittsburgh in the first round of the playoffs. With the game in overtime and Pittsburgh holding a 3-2 series lead, Martin Straka blew past a stumbling Gonchar for the winning tally and the end of Washington's season.

"It looked like he tripped over his own blueline," Rucki recalled.

> **"The guys were looking at me, going, 'What the hell was that?' "**
> **- Larry Murphy**

Because of that, and the fact he joined the hated Penguins in 2005 (he signed with Ottawa in 2010), Gonchar is greeted with a steady diet of whoops every time he makes a play.

"It's a constant until he stops touching the puck," Rucki said. "It's pretty consistent."

Rucki speculated players such as Gonchar and Murphy must know the chant is aimed at them, since it only occurs when they touch the puck. Sure enough, Gonchar has acknowledged the pastime, telling media members he considers it a "badge of honor," to be remembered in Washington, even if for derisive purposes.

And the fact Murphy is a Hall of Famer while Gonchar has a Stanley Cup ring and more than 800 points in his NHL career? That's a pretty good revenge, too.

PITTSBURGH PENGUINS
PHILADELPHIA FLYERS

It's right out of the wild, wild West, this four-decade rivalry between the Pittsburgh Penguins and Philadelphia Flyers. So it was fitting when former Penguins coach Herb Brooks invoked legendary outlaw Jesse James during a playoff series in 2000.

Pennsylvania's two teams have developed a ferocious hate for each other.

It happened after a late-game cheap shot, when Flyers defenseman Luke Richardson shot a puck from short range at Penguins defenseman Bob Boughner, who was wrestling with Keith Jones at center ice. The puck hit Boughner in the chest.

Brooks didn't mince words when asked about Richardson.

"I'd go back in his family tree," Brooks said. "Maybe he's a direct descendant of the guy that shot Jesse James in the back. You know, the coward that shot Jesse James in the back. It must be in his family tree. There's a code for tough guys in the league. This was way past the code."

Way past the code? That could describe an infinite number of incidents between these teams, each of which joined the NHL as part of 'The Expansion Six' in 1967-68.

But then, we assume you consider biting, stick-swinging and hallway arguments with coaches to be way past the code.

Let's sink our teeth into the alleged biting incidents first (yes, there are more than one).

In 2009, Flyers left winger Scott Hartnell appeared to take a munch out of Penguins defenseman Kris Letang's hand during a scrum along the boards.

"A first for me," Letang said, memorably.

Hartnell's take: "A lot of stuff happens on the bottom of the pile. He had his hands in my face, doing the face wash, and we were rolling around. I can't say what happened."

Funny, neither could Penguins left winger Matt Cooke when he was accused of biting Arron Asham in 2010.

"It's not bad, but he's a gutless guy," Asham said. "I have no respect for him at all. I lined up against him asked him to fight and he didn't want to. If you go and bite someone...He's garbage to me and I have no respect for him at all."

Let's move on to the hallway incident, shall we? It happened after an 8-2 Flyers victory in 2007, a game that featured 156 penalty minutes. Afterward, Flyers tough guy Ben Eager passed Penguins coach Michel Therrien in the hallway and said, "You're a joke." Therrien's two-word comeback is not printable here.

That was the same night 41-year-old Penguins left winger 'Scary' Gary Roberts beat the 23-year-old Eager to a pulp. Which is nothing compared to what Flyers goalie Ron Hextall wanted to do to Penguins winger Rob Brown during the 1989 Patrick Division final.

Brown had just completed a windmill fist-pump after putting the Penguins ahead 9-2, in what would become a 10-7 victory. Hextall lost his mind. He chased down Brown in Jason Voorhees-like fashion, goal stick above his head.

Brown took off like a frightened squirrel.

"Probably the quickest I've ever skated," he later said.

Finally, consider 'The Kaspar Krunch.' It happened on March 7, 1998, at the Civic Arena, when Penguins defenseman Darius Kasparaitis felled Flyers star Eric Lindros with a thunderous hit. A sell-out crowd cheered manically as Lindros crawled along the ice.

It so happened the teams played the next night in Philly. Robert Lang, who played for the Penguins that year, laughed as he recalled the rematch.

> "In one of my first games there I lost a couple of teeth."
> - Sidney Crosby

They got Kaspar on the first shift," he said.

That they did, legally mugging Kasparaitis behind the Penguins' net. He emerged from the attack with a smile on his face.

Penguins captain Sidney Crosby knew what he was getting into when he entered the NHL in 2005-06. He'd heard all about the bitterness on both sides.

"I was told," Crosby said. "I had seen (Penguins-Flyers) games before, and in one of my first games there, I lost a couple of teeth."

Penguins fans think the Flyers are brainless brutes, descendents not of Jesse James, but of the Broad Street Bullies of the 1970s, a championship outfit coached by Fred Shero, the late father of current Penguins GM Ray Shero.

Flyers fans think the Penguins are pretty boys. They despise Crosby, taunting him to no end each time he visits Wachovia Center.

"It's an intense building," he said.

"He's garbage to me and I have no respect for him at all.' - Arron Asham on Matt Cooke

The Flyers lead the all-time series, 132-83-30, though the Penguins have scored the biggest victories of late, eliminating the Flyers from the play-offs in 2008 and '09. The Penguins have won three Stanley Cups, the Flyers two.

But once upon a time, the Flyers owned the Penguins like few teams have ever owned another. Their dominance was highlighted by an unfathomable 39-0-3 steak at home over a 15-year span beginning in 1974.

"We were the dirt on the bottom of their shoes," recalled former Pittsburgh left winger Phil Bourque, now a Penguins broadcaster.

The streak finally ended on Feb. 2, 1989, at the Spectrum when Wendell Young, a former Flyer, made 39 saves in a 5-3 Penguins victory.

Three other memorable moments:

– On April 23, 1997, Mario Lemieux scored what many figured would be his last goal in Pittsburgh, in Game 4 of a playoff series against the Flyers (the Penguins trailed three games to none and had no plans to return to Pittsburgh for Game 6). "That was the first time I cried on the ice for a long time," Lemieux said.

– Philadelphia fans, notoriously hostile, twice showered Lemieux with standing ovations. The first came March 2, 1993, when he returned from a layoff after treatment for Hodgkin's disease. The second came April 26, 1997, when Lemieux played in what was thought to be his final game, a playoff series-ending loss to the Flyers.

– Former Penguin Ken Wregget, starting for an ailing Ron Hextall in Game 7 of the '89 playoff series, stoned the Pens in a 4-1 Flyers victory at the Civic Arena.

Finally, there was 'The Game,' or Game 4 of the Eastern Conference semifinal in 2000. It started May 4. It ended at 2:35 a.m. May 5, when Philly's Keith Primeau beat Ron Tugnutt on a wrist shot at 12:01 of the fifth overtime. That was the 72nd shot Tugnutt faced.

Afterward, then-Pens coach Brooks was asked to sum up the game. He managed a smile and said, "Where do you start, and where do you finish?"

The same could be said in attempting to describe a wild, wild rivalry that remains as hot as ever.

BRIAN BURKE
KEVIN LOWE

VS.

Brian Burke made a lot of headlines in his war of words with Kevin Lowe.

> ## "If I had run my team into the sewer like that I wouldn't throw a grenade at the other 29 teams."
> ## – Brian Burke

You know it's a good hissing contest when the league has to step in and break it up.

But what do you expect when a couple of short-fused battlers like Kevin Lowe and Brian Burke decide to drop the verbal gloves?

It was epic. Better stuff than fans saw on the ice a lot of nights. Fun while it lasted.

The two have since made up – realizing, after the death of Burke's son Brendan, that life is too short to waste on juvenile bickering – but when they did get into it, they got into it good.

It started in 2007 when Lowe, then GM of the Edmonton Oilers, pitched a five-year, $21.25 million offer sheet to Anaheim Ducks Group II restricted free agent Dustin Penner (and a bigger one to Buffalo's Thomas Vanek before that), which then-Anaheim GM Burke deemed reckless, unnecessary and irresponsible. Over and over and over.

He blamed Lowe for an escalation in player salaries and said he couldn't wait to cash in on the draft picks Edmonton handed over with the offer sheet because with Lowe running things, they were guaranteed to be high ones.

"(Players in their second contracts) are all being re-signed at inflated prices," Burke said. "Everything I said a year ago has come true. Every single word. Most managers don't like starting fights with any other managers. But you go right now from entry-level to what used to be the third contract, thanks to two offer sheets from Kevin Lowe."

He didn't stop there. Burke came at Lowe again, on TSN's 2007/08 season preview show.

"If I had run my team into the sewer like that I wouldn't throw a grenade at the other 29 teams and my own indirectly," Burke said. "So I have no intention of speaking to him anytime soon."

Lowe finally blew his stack, firing back in July 2008.

"Where do I begin?" Lowe asked. "He's a moron, first of all. He loves the limelight and I don't think anyone in hockey will dispute that. He's in a pathetic hockey market where they can't get on any page of the newspaper let alone the front page of the sports.

"This guy is an absolute media junkie and I guess he's achieving what he wants because he gets his name in the headlines. But I hate the fact that my name is linked to his. He's an underachieving wanna-be in terms of success in the NHL. He won a Stanley Cup? Great. I've won six Stanley Cups, you want to count rings? Who cares, it's just a little pathetic that he carries on.

"(Craig MacTavish) said it best – he's like the Wizard of Oz, you pull the curtains away and there's not much substance."

From a media perspective it was pure gold. The NHL didn't think so, however, and principal Gary Bettman called both men into the office and issued a cease and desist order.

That didn't mean they had put the feud behind them, though. For the next 18 months you could have played shinny on their icy relationship.

> "He's like the Wizard of Oz, you pull the curtains away and there's not much substance."
> - Kevin Lowe

It wasn't until tragedy struck that they finally ended the hostility. Brendan, before the car accident that claimed his life, told his father he and Lowe needed to make things right. When Lowe learned of Brendan's passing, he e-mailed Brian, offering his condolences. Burke called back immediately and made it known that he wanted to follow his son's wishes and mend the broken fence.

They came face to face for the first time at the Olympics in Vancouver, where they shook hands and hugged.

VS.

DANIEL ALFREDSSON
TORONTO

Senators captain Daniel Alfredsson is a pillar in the Ottawa community. He is revered for contributions and leadership on the ice and highly respected for his charity work around town. Alfredsson supports Right to Play, Boys and Girls Clubs and is a spokesperson for the Royal Ottawa Hospital.

Former NHL goalie turned television analyst Glenn Healy described Alfredsson "as much a gentleman as you can possibly get."

Yet, in the minds of many Toronto Maple Leafs fans, this mild-mannered, much-revered NHL veteran has been Public Enemy No. 1. Bar none.

Check out the popular website, Facebook, where Alfredsson is "hated by the power of 1,000 suns," by a group of Leafs lovers.

Alfredsson is booed relentlessly every time he touches the puck at Toronto's Air Canada Centre; has been ever since a controversial hit he administered to Darcy Tucker in the 2002 playoffs. The series and score were tied at two. In the waning moments, Alfredsson nudged or shoved Tucker from behind, depending from which fan perspective you viewed the hit. Seconds later with Tucker laying prone on the ice, Alfredsson proceeded to score the game-winning goal.

Looking back, even Alfredsson admits he may have gotten away with one.

> **"There will be fans that dislike me to a certain level."**
> **- Daniel Alfredsson**

"In today's game it would have been a penalty," Alfredsson said. "At the time they (the officials) probably didn't call a penalty as it was late in the third period of the playoffs."

Two seasons later, Alfredsson gave Leaf supporters another reason to jeer him. Toronto captain Mats Sundin had broken his stick in the previous game. In a fit of frustration Sundin tossed his stick over the glass into the crowd and was issued a one-game suspension for his carelessness.

Daniel Alfredsson's offensive prowess made him Public Enemy No. 1 whenever Ottawa visited Toronto.

With Sundin out of the lineup it was Alfredsson who was having stick issues. While on a scoring chance, Alfredsson's stick snapped. Instead of dropping his stick immediately, he looked up to the rafters and pretended to toss his stick in the air. Fans in attendance did not see the humor.

Alfredsson explained, "It wasn't planned. I had broken three, four sticks in the morning and three more in the game...It just happened to be in Toronto."

Alfredsson thought the incident was blown out of proportion and said "Sundin thought that it was funny."

Alfredsson has also gotten a rough ride from Leafs players on occasion. One particular incident from late in the 2007-08 season stands out. Toronto journeyman Mark Bell leveled Alfredsson with a heavy hit. With

Alfredsson on the ice "gasping for breath," Leaf fans cheered. Alfredsson sustained an MCL injury on the play, causing him to miss two playoff games. Until the '08 post-season, Alfredsson had appeared in every Senators playoff game.

Despite all of the constant catcalls from the Leaf throng to this day, Alfredsson does not harbor any ill will towards the Toronto fans.

> ## "Sundin thought it was funny."
> ## – Alfredsson on his broken stick gag

"Toronto fans are knowledgeable. They cheer for their team. I have no problems with their fans," he said. "There will be fans that dislike me to a certain level. When I walk in Toronto I feel nothing but respect towards me. There is nothing that bothers me."

VS. CANADIAN WOMEN
AMERICAN WOMEN

Canada's hockey rivalry with the United States extends into every permutation of the sport – including, and especially, the women's game.

And in case you thought the women's rivalry doesn't match the one between their male counterparts – because the women's game is smaller, and/or because many of the women from both countries play as teammates in the U.S. collegiate system – here's Hayley Wickenheiser to clarify the situation:

"Oh, for sure, I think there's still a bitter rivalry there," said Wickenheiser, longtime Team Canada captain and one of the greatest-ever female players. "There's no love lost between the two teams, and it's changed a bit in the sense that yeah, players play together on their NCAA teams, so some are friends.

"But when you step on the ice for Canada vs. The U.S., that feeling is still very much there. There's a genuine dislike or rivalry between the two teams that keeps it one of the better rivalries in sports."

"With their win-loss record, you have to respect the Canadians," added U.S. alternate captain Angela Ruggiero. "They play the game tough and hard, and that lends itself to stirring up emotions in their opponents. We're not any different. We expect neither side cares about anything other than winning."

The Canada/U.S. rivalry was intense long before 1998, when women's hockey was first played as an Olympic sport at the Nagano Winter Games. But that inaugural Olympic showdown for the gold medal – won 3-1 by the Americans, who went undefeated in the tournament – seemed to ratchet up the antipathy.

During the round-robin portion of those Games, the Canadian team was disgusted by American forward Sandra Whyte's alleged mocking of the recently deceased and Alzheimer's-stricken father of Team Canada forward Danielle Goyette.

The Vancouver Olympics featured yet another gold medal showdown between the Canadian and American women's teams.

Whyte denied the allegations – and at the next Winter Olympics (in Salt Lake City, Utah in 2002) the Americans would deny another allegation that angered Team Canada's players.

At that Olympic tournament, a rumor made the rounds that had the Americans placing a Canadian flag on their dressing room floor and stomping all over it. Again, the Americans were quick to dismiss the rumor, but judging by a passionate speech Wickenheiser made after Canada's gold medal victory, it was clear Team Canada was motivated by it.

> **"We expect neither side cares about anything other than winning."**
> **- Angela Ruggiero**

"The 2002 Games would be hard to top, in terms of emotion," Wickenheiser said eight years later. "The whole feeling during those Olympics was us against the world almost, and being in the U.S. when Sept. 11 had recently happened, it was a very emotionally charged game, and very different from (the 2010 Winter Olympics in) Vancouver."

Ah, yes, the 2010 Vancouver Games. The women's hockey portion of those Games was won by Team Canada – its third consecutive gold medal – in a 2-0 win.

Again, the rivalry between two of hockey's greatest nations revealed itself – this time at the medals ceremonies after Canada's win.

When they received their silver medals, many of the American women cried quietly. Some people attempted to chide the emotional U.S. team for what they labeled as poor sportsmanship when they'd just won a silver medal.

But, at least for once, Wickenheiser jumped to the defense of her rivals.

"That's kind of a really ignorant comment in a way because you don't really 'win' a silver medal in hockey – you lose the gold," Wickenheiser said. "I've been at that stage back in '98, and at some World Championships, and it's devastating. It's just hard to switch gears and think to yourself, 'wow, I won a silver medal'.

"I don't think I would've been any different; I would've been quite upset, because of all the work that goes into everything and how invested you are. It's almost like the death of something when that happens."

The death of a particular dream, absolutely. But the rivalry between the Canadian women and their American counterparts will be around for quite some time.

"Every game we play against them is always going to matter," Wickenheiser said. "We want to continue to grow the game and eventually develop better rivalries with teams like Sweden and Finland. But there's no doubt that with all that's happened between us already, the (U.S./Canada) rivalry is only going to get better."

DOUG HARVEY
THE HOCKEY HALL OF FAME

VS.

For the record, the only person to turn down nomination for the Hall of Fame was former NHL president Gil Stein, who did so after it was learned that he had helped engineer his own induction in 1993.

Doug Harvey was a dominant defenseman, so why was his trip to the Hall of Fame delayed?

But 20 years prior to that, Doug Harvey made his own emphatic statement concerning the Hall of Fame, a principle from which he never wavered when it came to one of the game's most hallowed institutions. The truth is, Harvey never wanted any part of a Hall of Fame that judged his actions off the ice.

Harvey never acknowledged his induction and did not attend the ceremony. The Hall still has the letter from Harvey's ex-wife, Ursula, which politely informed the Hall of Fame that Harvey had not changed his stance on his decision to refuse induction. It also still has the ring that is traditionally presented to each inductee because Harvey never bothered to pick it up.

It is a rivalry that will likely never be quelled because Harvey died of cirrhosis of the liver in 1989. Unless one of his family members decides to bury the hatchet, it's likely Harvey will always be at odds with the Hall of Fame.

Was Harvey a Hall of Fame defenseman? Well, considering that he was the best defenseman of his generation and, depending upon who's giving the opinion, the greatest blueliner of all-time, that's a given. Harvey won seven Norris Trophies in eight years, was a pivotal figure in six Stanley Cups with the Montreal Canadiens and was a first-team all-star 10 times.

> **"They won't put me in because I'm not averse to sampling the nectar of the gods now and then."**
> **- Doug Harvey**

So, yeah, he was a Hall of Famer.

But Harvey also had a tragic flaw. He had a drinking problem that some think was the result of bipolar disorder and depression that was diagnosed too late in his life. Tales of Harvey's drinking were sometimes as legendary as what he did on the ice. Harvey once told a reporter that when he died, his body would not decompose for a long time because, "It's full of alcohol. It's got its own embalming fluid."

And it's why the Hall of Fame refused to induct him in 1972 after the customary three-year wait had lapsed for Harvey. Former Canadiens GM Frank Selke, who was a member of the Hall of Fame's selection

"I'll hoist a few in full view of everyone."
- Harvey

committee, essentially told Harvey he had been turned down because of his drinking.

So when the Hockey Hall of Fame decided to induct him the next season, Harvey took so much umbrage with what had transpired the year before that he refused to have anything to do with his induction and on the day of the ceremony went fishing instead. He was also upset that it took the Hall of Fame so long to induct former Maple Leafs star Busher Jackson, who had also fallen on hard times because of alcoholism. Jackson retired in 1944, but wasn't inducted until 1971.

"What they're telling me is that they won't put me in because I'm not averse to sampling the nectar of the gods now and then," Harvey said at the time. "The difference is that I'll hoist a few in full view of everyone where other guys will sneak around the corner to do theirs."

CONN SMYTHE

FRANK SELKE

VS.

One of the best trades in Toronto Maple Leafs history also brought to a head one of the franchise's all-time rifts.

From the late 1920s through the latter stages of the '50s, very little happened in Leafland without the approval of Conn Smythe. On the most basic level, Smythe was simply the boss and one of his shrewdest moves in that role came early on in his tenure when he brought an astute young hockey mind named Frank Selke into the Toronto fold.

There was a definite kinship between the two men, who were bound by a common passion for the game and spotting players who really knew how to play it.

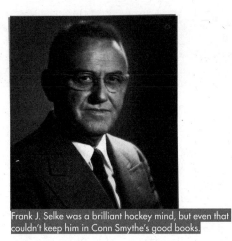

Frank J. Selke was a brilliant hockey mind, but even that couldn't keep him in Conn Smythe's good books.

"There was a real camaraderie there, there was a real partnership and I think there was a mutual admiration," said Kevin Shea, director of publications and online features for the Hockey Hall of Fame. "They both knew Toronto-area hockey like no other and I think that's one of the reasons they banded together."

One of Selke's earliest and largest contributions to the organization came via his employment history as an electrician. Leveraging the union connections he made plying that trade, Selke was instrumental in getting Maple Leaf Gardens built when most doubted it would ever happen.

Job titles back in those days weren't as rigid as they are now, but suffice it to say Selke was Smythe's right-hand man.

To that end, when Smythe departed to lead troops in Europe during the Second World War, Selke was left in charge of hockey personnel decisions, with the understanding all transactions would be subject to final approval from afar by Smythe.

In September of 1943, Selke moved to acquire a young center named Ted Kennedy from the Montreal Canadiens in exchange for defenseman Frank Eddolls, whose rights the Habs had previously traded to the Leafs three years earlier.

According to lore, Selke made a failed attempt to connect with Smythe. After consulting with another prominent member of Leafs management, Hap Day, and believing the trade was one that simply must be made, Selke went ahead with the deal that landed Toronto one of its best players in franchise history.

"He talks to his advisors, including Day and makes the deal," Shea said. "And Smythe goes ballistic, even though it turned out to be the greatest deal, certainly of that era (for the Leafs)."

To Smythe, who valued loyalty above all, Selke was making a play in his absence to seize control of the Leafs. Not particularly caring for the accusation and increasingly fed up working for such an authoritarian, Selke allegedly scribbled something to the effect of, 'Lincoln freed the slaves 80 years ago. Thanks very much; it's been nice working for you.'

Whether that was just Selke's way of saving face after being fired is irrelevant. All that matters is, in 1946, he moved into the GM's chair in Montreal and set about building the farm system he'd begun to put in place in Toronto.

Given Selke's mind for the game and drive to succeed, perhaps his feud with Smythe only expedited what was an inevitable separation.

"Selke was a talented guy and his talent was never going to be recognized or realized in Toronto," said D'Arcy Jenish, a hockey historian who authored *The Montreal Canadiens: 100 Years of Glory*. "He got the perfect job, perfect employer in Senator Donat Raymond. The board in Montreal gave Selke a clear mandate. They just wanted a good team. The famous line was, 'Go ahead and build an empire.'"

Much of the work Selke had done with the Leafs came to fruition when the team won four Cups in five years between 1947 and 1951. The fact Toronto was winning in the immediate aftermath of his move masked how important the shift was. But once the Habs started reaping the rewards of Selke's far-reaching feeder system, his ability to build high-end teams became blatantly apparent.

Smythe and Selke were able to co-exist as GMs in a six-team league, even working together on the creation of the Hockey Hall of Fame in 1961. In essence, the two were just a contrast in personalities, Selke the more measured man, while Smythe always saw things in distinct shades.

"Smythe was hot and cold," Shea said. "It was black, it was white and it was never grey. Different personalities, for sure."

> "It was black, it was white and it was never grey."
> - Kevin Shea

VS. AHL
IHL

One of hockey's most heated rivalries through much of the 1990s involved neither individuals nor teams, but leagues, as the American and International circuits staged an all-out turf war at the top level of minor-league hockey.

History has judged the right and wrong moves – burdened by expenses that outscored revenues, the original IHL collapsed in 2001 – but while the rivalry burned, there was no shortage of agitation across league lines.

"It was pretty acrimonious at times and there were a couple of forays where the IHL or the commissioner of the day decided they would step out and offer us the opportunity to merge with them," said AHL president and CEO Dave Andrews. "I was offered the opportunity to be the hockey guy and they would be the business people."

But based on what Andrews knew about both businesses, specifically that the IHL was being propped up by unheard-of, $5-million expansion fees in the early '90s, he declined.

At the height of its growth, the 19-team IHL even fancied itself as a rival to the NHL.

> "Major-league expenses with minor-league revenues. That was a big part of the story."
> - Doug Moss

"I remember those days and everybody thinking that our league was spending a lot of time on the entertainment side of things," said Grand Rapids Griffins GM Bob McNamara, who previously worked for Cleveland's IHL franchise. " 'Affordable entertainment,' that was a big catch-phrase.

"It was a real, real rapid expansion into markets that didn't make a lot of sense for hockey. I'm not into taking shots at people, but it expanded too quickly and certain people felt we could be a league that could draw from NHL fans. That was obviously a big mistake."

The Manitoba Moose were one of the franchises taken on by the American League when the International League folded.

Before it went away after an 11-team final season in 2000-01, the IHL had realized some error in its ways, re-engaging with the NHL for affiliations and player placement.

The spring of 1999 marked another hot flash, one that worried the more stable AHL, when the NHL's Ottawa Senators got a better deal and placed their farm team with IHL Grand Rapids, when they already owned a franchise in the AHL.

"Our suspension fee was $15,000, so that made it easy for Ottawa to go elsewhere," said Andrews, who acted quickly, escalating those fees to prevent any other defectors. "We battled in several markets and that was the only one we lost."

Not long after that blow, Andrews admits to having little tolerance for showing further AHL weakness. Answering questions at the all-star game about any potential co-operation between the leagues, he shot back, "Why would you want to get together with someone who's trying to eat your lunch?"

The question was about the chatter that the leagues were considering a common all-star game.

"That was not on," said IHL Manitoba Moose governor Mark Chipman about the rebuff. "We were the pursuers and it was like, 'Take your all-star game and...' "

Added McNamara: "I think they saw our league as an affront to their league's existence. We probably never realized how bitter a rivalry it was until we moved into the AHL."

Andrews is not shy about what was at stake.

"It was a struggle for survival," Andrews said. "We had to move very quickly to stake out a piece of the landscape...even if we didn't have the financial depth of ownership it appeared the IHL was developing and market strength they were developing."

Within the business, competition for players was often fierce, stoked by agents looking to place more experienced veterans.

"I don't think there's any question that at that time, the IHL's salary scale was higher than the AHL's," said Hershey Bears GM Doug Yingst. "More often than not you'd lose out."

AHL executives' suspicions about their IHL rivals were often close to the mark.

"We wondered on the business side how they could continue with travel expenses," Yingst said. "At the end of the day, as good as that league was, that's what did them in. And I think what we found later was that the IHL teams hated the IHL teams more than the hate between leagues."

In the end, the IHL was a fractured group. Some governors were losing money, others were just going their separate ways and wanted out. There were suspended franchises and others who did and didn't want NHL affiliation.

"It was a great league with some great games and great rivalries," said the final IHL commissioner, Doug Moss, who only joined the league in 1998. "But I think the handwriting was on the wall. There was a lot of travel, major-league expenses with minor-league revenues. That was a big part of the story."

Andrews said there was little actual subterfuge over time, though he did admit to reading the odd fax mistakenly given to him, but intended for

David Andrews, the former Hartford Whalers executive who spent a few years as the IHL's senior vice-president of business operations.

Both Andrews and Moss said that in the final chapters, the acrimony subsided.

The end game to the rivalry was that the best plan won out. Andrews had cast an early die in his first months on the job in 1994. He saw an immediate need for a clearer player-development identity to make the AHL more attractive to the NHL. His league's CBA with minor-league players had expired on his arrival and, against the players' wishes, he implemented the development rule on rosters, restricting the number of veteran players.

The players fought him all the way to the National Labor Relations Board and lost (no player from the previous season was found to have lost employment because of the rule) and the AHL had its development mission.

"I think they saw our league as an affront to their league's existence."
- Bob McNamara

"We knew our own knitting," Andrews said. "We just had to get better at it. So we said we'll be a dedicated player-development league for the NHL and we're going to be the best one."

The final solution on the IHL side – that Grand Rapids, Chicago, Milwaukee, Utah, Houston and Manitoba joined the AHL as expansion teams in 2001 – was mostly negotiated in secret by Chipman and Milwaukee governor Francis Croak.

Equally clandestine, Andrews fashioned the deal for the previously 20-team AHL, eventually paving the way for the 2010 achievement of 30 AHL teams for 30 NHL teams.

VS. CALGARY FLAMES
EDMONTON OILERS

There's the old story about the hockey fan asking his Calgary friend what he was going to do after the Edmonton Oilers advanced to the 2006 Stanley Cup final to face the Carolina Hurricanes.

"You have to cheer for the Alberta team, don't you?" he asked. "I can't imagine you'll be cheering for Carolina."

"Are you kidding?" the Calgarian responds. "If the Oilers were playing the Taliban all-stars, I'd be painting Al-Qaeda banners to take to the game."

Gross hyperbole, to be sure, but welcome to the Battle of Alberta. This is what it is – a pure, unadulterated out-and-out hate for the other team in the province. There's no love lost because it was never there to begin with.

"It goes way back before the Flames and Oilers," said Hall of Famer and former Flame Lanny McDonald, a native of Hanna in south central Alberta. "In football, it was the Stampeders and Eskimos who fought for the bragging rights between the two cities and that goes back many decades.

"Edmonton is the capital. We – I hate to say we, but – Calgary always considered themselves the big boys always trying to prove their worth. When Edmonton came into the league (from the World Hockey Association in 1979) and Calgary transferred from Atlanta (in 1980), it didn't take long to heat up. Those are the great things in sport. You're doing everything possible not to let your team or the city down. And you know your friends are going to give it to you if you lose to the bad guys."

The rivalry between the cities surely dates back a century when the oil-rich deposits around Calgary began boosting its economy and it started to compete on a variety of levels with the provincial capital and administrative hub of Edmonton. In sports, senior hockey teams from the two cities sparked a competitive wedge, then pro football arrived in Calgary in 1948 and Edmonton a year later. But the moniker 'Battle of Alberta' wasn't created until the NHL arrived in the 1980s.

"The first season in the old Corral, I can remember Dave Semenko going over and trying to spear one of the Calgary players at the Calgary bench," said longtime Oilers play-by-play man Rod Phillips. "That was the first season the two teams played against each other. It started right

Calgary's Jarome Iginla takes on Edmonton's Sheldon Souray in a familar sight for Alberta hockey fans.

off the get-go. They were always very, very tough hard-played angry games...all of them."

After a couple of growing years, the Oilers dominated not just the rivalry with Calgary, but the entire NHL. And that forced the Flames to become stronger. The Battle of Alberta intensity level went off the charts in the '80s, when the Oilers won five Stanley Cups in a seven-year stretch and the Flames won once and lost in the final another year. The head-to-head battles were epic.

The Edmonton dynasty was led by Hall of Famers Wayne Gretzky, Mark Messier, Jari Kurri, Paul Coffey, Glenn Anderson, Grant Fuhr and coach-GM architect Glen Sather. But it was warriors such as Dave Semenko,

Marty McSorley, Don Jackson, Kevin McClelland, Lee Fogolin, Dave Hunter and Esa Tikkanen who kept the rivalry spirited and physical.

The Flames had a number of premier players themselves, such as McDonald, Joe Nieuwendyk, Joe Mullen, Doug Gilmour, Al MacInnis and others. And they also had a strong cast of soldiers who did the dirty work in the trenches; Joel Otto, Jim Peplinski, Tim Hunter and Doug Risebrough to name a few.

"Because Edmonton had become successful, there needed to be a team from Calgary that tried to stick with them," Otto said. "Gretzky was very difficult to stop. Our strategy was to do whatever we could to get Messier off his game. And that opportunity for me got me in the league. Calgary was looking for a big center. I couldn't match his skill, but I could be physical with him."

Said Phillips: "Messier and Otto were like two bull rams running at each other for many years."

When regards for one another were at their worst, the Battle of Alberta went on around the clock, 12 months a year, not just the length of the hockey season.

"The level of hatred was pretty high," said Calgary play-by-play man Peter Maher. "I used to be involved in a charity summer golf tournament in Red Deer for Special Olympics. My job was to get celebrities for it. In those days you could get five guys from each side to go. But they never inter-mixed. The Calgary guys stayed on their side and the Oiler guys stayed on their side. They never mixed. They'd have the dinner the night before and it was pretty clear, keep them separate."

The Battle of Alberta in the '80s went beyond provincial borders. Calgary-Edmonton games were highly anticipated as television spectacles on *Hockey Night In Canada* and TSN. Said Phillips: "The whole country couldn't wait for a Calgary-Edmonton game because they were great battles. They hated each other."

Locally, you could forget about buying tickets for those games. You'd be lucky to even get into a sports bar unless you showed up well in advance. Even the players admit the encounters were truly special.

"People used to ask 'Do you look at the schedule and mark down when those six or eight games are?' " McDonald recalled. "I'd say, 'no, it's just part of the schedule. One game is as important as the next.' Those are the things you're supposed to say.

"Heck, in reality, I had them Xed off as soon as the schedule came out. You knew when they were going to be playing you. You geared up for it. Even though you never said it, you knew exactly when the next game was."

With every rivalry, there's a level of respect for the opponent. Or so they say. Was their even a shred or moral value between a Flame and an Oiler? In a way, there was.

"They'd go out of their way to avoid each other. It was engrained in their fibers back then." - Peter Maher

"There's definitely a respect factor because in this case, they were the guys owning the Cups and we were the guys chasing," McDonald said. "(Flames coach) Bob Johnson did a phenomenal job in the 1980s preparing us not only to win the Cup, but build a foundation to find a way to beat Edmonton. He always said if we found a way to beat Edmonton, we'd have a great chance to win the Stanley Cup."

That almost happened in 1985-86. The Oilers were favored to win their third Cup in a row, but lost to Calgary in a second-round series when Edmonton defenseman Steve Smith scored into his own net in the third period of Game 7. Calgary went on to the final before losing to Montreal. After Edmonton rebounded for Cup wins in 1987 and '88, Calgary won one of its own in 1989.

The intensity of this provincial rivalry waned in the 1990s as the Oilers dealt off their assets and the team missed the playoffs four straight seasons. The Flames went through a rebuilding phase as well, in which they made the playoffs just once in a nine-year run starting in the late 1990s. Sure, the Alberta squads wanted to beat each other, but it's tough to get a big hate-on for a fellow crappy team.

"They've never matched that intensity level from the 1980s," Maher said. "I don't think it will ever get to that level again. The players' mindset today is so much different. Nowadays, you see after games Flames guys talking to the Oilers guys while they're waiting to get on the bus. You'd never see that in the '80s. They'd go out of their way to avoid each other. It was engrained in their fibers back then."

The Battle of Alberta rivalry absolutely spills over the boards and envelops the fan. When Calgary went to the Cup final versus Tampa Bay in 2004, some of the more open-minded hockey fans in Edmonton caused a big controversy. A handful of them actually had the gall to cheer for the team representing their province.

"There were a number of people in Edmonton who put on those Flames car flags as a show of support for Calgary," Maher said. "And some people, especially the talk shows, took offense to that. I remember all the talk about the Edmonton fans being called turncoats for cheering for the Flames. And they'd counter saying they're just cheering for the team from our province, from our country.

"Then when the Oilers went to the final in 2006, here in Calgary, there was the odd person who adopted Edmonton and had car flags with the Oilers on them. Hard to believe, but they could have been Edmontonians just passing through town."

The Flames and Oilers shared little in common over the years, so suffice it to say, they weren't going to be trading partners. That changed in 2009-10 when defenseman Steve Staios became the first player to get traded from one team to another, landing in Calgary after eight seasons in Edmonton.

"We're all professionals," Staios said at the time. "I have no problem going into that dressing room. I couldn't say this when I was with the Oilers, but I have a high amount of respect for the Flames organization."

Maybe the world is changing.

VS. CANADA RUSSIA

In the history of international sport, few if any rivalries match the mythology that has grown up around Canada versus Russia in hockey. Dominations and meltdowns. Boycotts. The Summit Series. The Super Series. Canada Cups. The Punch-up in Piestany. All have helped create an aura like none other surrounding the two hockey superpowers. Competitiveness? Intensity? Both are hallmarks of Canada-Russia encounters, but it is the romanticism underlying it all that has kept the rivalry alive for seven decades.

Since the fall of the Iron Curtain in 1989, globalization of the game and a pacification of global politics have taken some of the edge off the rivalry, the intrigue surrounding the contests now involves 'who will win?' not 'who are these guys?'

But it wasn't always that way. There was a time when Canada was virtually unbeatable in hockey. From 1920 to 1952, the Canucks won every Olympic gold medal save for one – 1936, when a Great Britain team stocked with Canadians was victorious. And from 1930 to 1952, Canada won 10 of the 12 world championships it entered. But when the Soviet Union joined the international hockey scene, it was like aliens had landed.

Much more than hockey was on the line when the Soviet Union and Canada clashed in 1972.

In 1954, the USSR made its first appearance at the World Championship – and won. The Soviets finished with a 6-0-1 record and a plus-27 goal differential; Canada won silver. And an on-ice dogfight was born. The Canucks bounced back the next year, claiming gold and out-scoring their opponents by 60 goals, including a 5-0 pasting of the Soviets in the gold-medal game, but that marked the end of Canadian trounces.

In 1956, the Soviets ended Canada's Olympic run – and began the Great White North's 50-year drought – by winning gold at the Cortina d'Ampezzo (Italy) Games. During the 1960s, '70s and '80s, Soviet domination and Canadian frustration continued. From 1963 to 1993 the USSR won 26 gold medals at world championships and Olympics and 33 medals overall.

The USSR's domination was so overwhelming Canada boycotted international play during the 1970s. The Canadians contended the Soviet players were professionals playing amateur tournaments. The protest kept Canada out of the 1972 and '76 Olympic Games and seven world championships. The acrimony grew.

While Canada's national amateur sides were missing competitions, Canadians in general were infuriated and embarrassed by the fact they could no longer lay claim to world hockey supremacy.

"I was out to prove that this was our sport," said Canadian defenseman Brad Park. "We developed it and we'd been taking a kicking from the Soviets in international hockey for a while, and if we had our best players we could show you what we can do."

And that bruised – or, rather, battered – ego gave rise to the seminal moment in international hockey history, the 1972 Summit Series.

Canada saw the series as a chance at redemption – to prove once and for all its on-ice superiority. The Soviets saw it as a chance at vindication – to prove their perceived professionals could beat the best the cocky Canadians had to offer.

Most fans know the history: Canadians – including the players themselves – figured the series would be a walkover; an eight-game warm-up for the upcoming NHL season with a nice Swedish vacation tossed in for good measure. It was, of course, anything but.

Eventually won 4-3-1 by Canada, the series was a back-and-forth affair that surprised everyone – except, presumably, the Soviets – with how competitive it was.

"I think early in the '70s with the Canada Cup and the '72 and '74 series, everyone realized very quickly how good these players were," said Lanny McDonald, who played in the 1976 Canada Cup. "We were going to have our hands full."

The Summit Series became a political and patriotic tour de force that changed the face of hockey forever and is remembered – however romantically – as some of the greatest hockey ever played.

"By the time we left Canada, our backs were against the wall," Park said. "The media had basically taken a lot of shots at us, the Canadian people were unhappy; the Russians looked like the good guys, we looked like assholes."

But for the players, the series wasn't a political event until it shifted to Moscow.

Park, who referred to his then 24-year-old self as "political as a Golden Retriever," said the series became political – personal, really – when the games shifted to Moscow. Food was rationed, beer went missing, in-room intercoms suddenly played music in the middle of the night, crank calls were regular happenings and run-ins with the Soviet military were not uncommon. The guys were able to deal with those distractions, but when it came to the wives who had made the trip, no quarter was given.

While in Sweden for two weeks before heading to Moscow, the Canadians got word that their wives would have to stay in a different hotel in Moscow. Poor treatment like that continued once the Canadians landed in Russia.

"That's when it started to get political," Park said. "The wives were treated like shit."

That, of course, wasn't what the public saw. It saw a battle of titans on the ice; two styles that couldn't have been more different – free-flowing, puck-controlling, stoic Soviets vs. crash-and-bang, ankle-breaking, emotional Canadians. The entire series became a metaphor for the Cold War.

Denis Potvin played in the 1976 and '81 Canada Cup tourneys. He remembers the Soviets as very different from the brash, outgoing, even cocky stars of the NHL people know today.

"They were very much under the Iron Curtain, the thumb of the Red Army," Potvin said. "So you didn't have that kind of swagger.

"They were very different, I mean, they were controlled. As great hockey players as they were, they just came from a whole different regime, whereas now Ovechkin and all those guys they were born free, basically."

The Canadians, meanwhile, were led on the ice in 1972 by the passionate Phil Esposito, who laid bare his soul to interviewer Johnny Esaw on national television after Game 4 in Vancouver, pleading with Canadians to back their boys. The take-no-prisoners Harry Sinden was coach with former NHL tough guy John Ferguson his assistant. The Canadian contingent also included the bombastic Don Cherry and Alan Eagleson, best remembered for flipping the bird to Russian fans in Moscow.

As was written in the pages of THN all those years ago: "It was almost impossible to describe the emotion that gripped the Moscow Sports Palace.

"The 3,000 Canadian fans who were over for the games were hysterical at the finish and they never let the Russians forget for a minute that they had won it all."

> ## "I knew when we were in a sort of 'us against the world' kind of thing."
> ## - Denis Potvin

In the years that followed the Summit Series, the best of Canada and the Soviet Union clashed more often; not at the Olympics or world championship, but in club and international exhibitions, although they weren't treated as such by the players.

In 1974, the second – and considerably less-billed – Summit Series was played between Canadian World Hockey Association players and the Soviet national side. And during the 1975-76 season, the Red Army and Soviet Wings club teams traveled to North America and played the 'Super Series' against eight NHL teams. The New Year's Eve contest between the Red Army and the Montreal Canadiens is still considered one of the greatest games ever played.

In 1976, the inaugural Canada Cup – featuring the best from Canada, the USSR, Czechoslovakia, Sweden, Finland and the U.S. – was won by Canada. A second place finish in '81 was followed by three more titles for the Canucks, with one win and a runner-up going to the USSR. The two bitter rivals met twice in Cup final, splitting them.

The Canada Cup featured the world's best until the final tournament in 1991. Bobby Orr, Vladislav Tretiak and Wayne Gretzky were three of the tournament's MVPs and set the stage for professionals at the Olympics.

"I knew when we were in a sort of 'us against the world' kind of thing," said Potvin, a Hall of Famer and three-time Norris Trophy winner of the '76 Canada Cup. "And it wasn't just the Russians, we had the Czechs – those teams that came from the 'dark side,' the Iron Curtain."

During the turbulent 1970s, Summit Series, Super Series and Canada Cups set the stage for the biggest rivalry in hockey history. Those competitions created the legend that is Russia vs. Canada.

"No question," said Hall of Famer Michel Goulet, who played in the 1984 and '87 Canada Cups, "1972 was really the start of it."

In recent years, Canada and the U.S. have forged what some consider to be *the* international hockey rivalry of the 21st century. But even if Canada-Russia is a little less heated than in years past, a game between the two still boils blood in both nations.

It's a struggle for supremacy that was forged in the 1970s and will live for as long as hockey lives.

"They're still Russians, we're still Canadians," Potvin said. "It's still there, whatever there means."

SIDNEY CROSBY
ALEX OVECHKIN

VS.

One is the son of an Olympic champion, the other the progeny of a junior goalie who never made it to the NHL. One grew up amidst the bright lights of one of the biggest cities in the world, the other in small-town Nova Scotia. One has a slightly bigger bank account and individual trophy case, the other an Olympic gold medal and a Stanley Cup to keep him warm at night.

Perhaps the greatest thing about Alex Ovechkin and Sidney Crosby is that it's a rivalry only in its infancy. Assuming both players manage to avoid serious injuries, we could be treated to them going hammer and tong for another 10 or 15 years.

The truth of the matter is that Crosby and Ovechkin don't really know each other very well. They've only met a handful of times off the ice and their on-ice meetings haven't exactly resulted in sparks flying all over the place. It's not like they meet in the corner and growl at one another or try to take each other's knees out in the neutral zone.

No, the beauty of this rivalry is in the traits possessed by those who are involved. Both sublimely talented, both with levels of passion that go off the scales, both with the willingness to drive the net, both with the capacity and the desire to be difference-makers.

> "It's like asking me if I'm going to be best friends with five guys on the Flyers."
> - Sidney Crosby

In their first five seasons in the league, both players had eclipsed the 100-point mark four times. They were separated by a total of just 23 points. To be sure, Crosby has been far more successful in terms of team achievements, but Ovechkin has something Crosby will never, ever be able to get. He won the Calder Trophy over Crosby in 2005-06.

All told, over the course of their first five seasons in the league, Ovechkin and Crosby have gone head-to-head a total of 26 times, including playoffs. (Crosby missed one regular season game with an injury.) The Penguins won the first 10 of 11 regular season meetings before the Capitals went on a run that saw them win seven of the next eight. The Penguins, of course, bettered the Capitals in the second round of the playoffs in 2009. In the 26 meetings, Crosby had 20 goals and 46 points, Ovechkin 23 goals and 42 points.

There have been times when the two have briefly sniped at one another on the ice and off, with the most intense exchange coming in a 5-2 Washington win Feb. 22, 2009. Neither seemed terribly impressed with the other, but it was still fairly tame and civil.

Prior to the game, Crosby and the Penguins said they felt an Ovechkin hit on Crosby in the previous meeting was dirty. Commenting on Crosby's penchant for yapping and talking to officials, Ovechkin said, "What can I say about him? He is a good player, but he talks too much. I play hard. If he wants to do something like hit me again, try to hit me again – and I'll talk to you guys (about) who plays dirty. That's not my game. It's not cheap shots, it's a game moment. But if he doesn't like it, it's his problem."

Crosby responded by saying that he was less than impressed with Ovechkin's goal celebrations.

Sidney Crosby and Alex Ovechkin are already forever linked by their skills and rivalry.

"Like it or lump it, that's what he does," Crosby said. "Some people like it, some people don't. Personally, I don't like it."

But for the most part, the real magnificence in the rivalry lies in what the two accomplish on the 200-by-85 foot sheet of frozen water. An example of their brilliance in that respect came in Game 2 of the '09 playoffs, when both players scored hat tricks in a 4-3 Washington win.

"The only thing I can honestly say is that if people can take anything out of this," Crosby said, "I hope they see it's the passion we have."

Even if they display it in different ways. When Ovechkin scores a big goal, everyone in the world knows about it. He often hurls himself against the glass back-first or, as was the case when he scored his 50th in 2008-09, choreographs a celebration that does not go over well with those in the hockey establishment who take themselves far too seriously.

Could you ever see Crosby making like his stick is on fire? Most of the time, you'll simply see him pull the mouthguard out of his mouth and open his arms to his teammates. There's a clear demarcation here. Even in goal celebrations, Ovechkin is far more the individual, while Crosby can't seem to wait to celebrate with his teammates. There isn't necessarily anything wrong with either of them, but it does illustrate some differences in character.

It will be interesting to see where this all goes in the coming years, particularly if Crosby continues to better Ovechkin when it comes to team success. There's no indication either franchise is about to go on a decline in the coming years, so it's a good bet the two will find themselves sharing large stages in the future.

One of the things that makes the rivalry so good is the fact that not only do the two seem to rise to the occasion almost every time, neither one is a perimeter player and will never fade into the background.

> **"I respect him as a person. But when I step on the ice, I respect only my teammates."**
> **- Alex Ovechkin**

When asked about his feelings about Ovechkin, Crosby said he certainly doesn't hold any ill will toward Ovechkin, but they're not about to start exchanging birthday cards, either.

"It's like asking me if I'm going to be best friends with five guys on the Flyers," Crosby said. "That's probably not going to happen. To say we absolutely hate each other, I don't think so, but we're competitive guys and that's kind of the result of everything and how it's been built up."

When asked the same question, Ovechkin replied, "I respect him as a person. But when I step on the ice, I respect only my teammates."

ERIC LINDROS
QUEBEC

Eric Lindros indicated it was just business, not personal.

And the Quebec Nordiques were exactly that – all business, when it came to hating Lindros for personal reasons.

When hockey's most ballyhooed prospect since (pick one) – Mario Lemieux, Wayne Gretzky, Bobby Orr – proclaimed he wouldn't play for Marcel Aubut's Nordiques, it set off a firestorm the likes of which had not been seen since the Battle of the Plains of Abraham in the French and Indian War in 1759.

The Nordiques had the first pick of the 1991 draft and decided to use it on Lindros anyway.

After Lindros' pronouncement of his intentions not to play in Quebec, anti-Eric sentiment in Quebec grew ugly.

"There were cartoons of Eric dressed up as a Ku Klux Klan member," recalled Carl Lindros, Eric's father. "It turned into a political and racial thing that was never intended."

Draft day was a nightmare for phenom prospect Eric Lindros.

Lindros spent the 1991-1992 season playing for the Canadian national team, which included participation in the '92 Winter Olympics at Lillehammer, Norway. When it became clear he would stick to his guns about not playing in Quebec, the Nordiques decided to trade him to the Flyers at the '92 draft.

> **"We wondered if they might actually try to kill Eric. That's how nuts it got."**
> **- Kerry Huffman**

Aubut made one last pitch before shopping his prized prospect.

"The argument would be made 'Eric, come to Quebec City and you will be a god,' " Carl Lindros said. "Eric never wanted to be a god."

Lindros himself could never see himself in a long-term relationship with the Nordiques.

"In the middle of one of our meetings," he said, "(Aubut) said to my parents, 'If your kid grew up in Quebec, he'd be a better person.' Once, he told me he wanted me for life. All I could picture is me with (prison) stripes on my shirt."

The controversial trade (which had to be finalized through arbitration because Aubut had made proposals to both the Flyers and New York Rangers) came at a steep price to Philadelphia: Peter Forsberg, Ron Hextall, Mike Ricci, Steve Duchesne, Kerry Huffman, Chris Simon, two No. 1 draft picks and $15 million.

That deal made headlines for days and weeks but the fun was just getting started for 'The Next One.'

At the start of the '92 season, things were going smoothly in Philadelphia but there was still the sticky matter of returning to the scene of the crime, namely Quebec City, to face the Nordiques at Le Colisee.

Coach Bill Dineen wisely sat out Lindros for an exhibition game but when the Flyers returned for a regular-season encounter, the public outcry was overwhelming.

Hundreds of grown men showed up for the game wearing diapers, bonnets and bibs, waving rattles at No. 88, whose refusal to play fueled tension between the French- and English citizens of Quebec.

"Those people in Quebec were really passionate and the hatred they had for Eric was incredible," Huffman recalled. "Even the days leading up to the game were a circus.

"Hexy, Ricci and I were talking before the game and we wondered if they might actually try to kill Eric. That's how nuts it got."

Adding to the maelstrom was a local radio station's decision to distribute thousands of baby pacifiers, which were promptly tossed onto the ice.

"That was wild," Dineen recalled. "It was the craziest thing I'd ever seen at a hockey game."

BOB PROBERT
TIE DOMI

VS.

Bob Probert (left) and Tie Domi had some of the most hyped and talked-about fights in hockey history.

It was a battle so big, it often eclipsed the hockey game itself. Two of the most feared and revered fighters of the era, Bob Probert and Tie Domi went at each other with gusto nine times during their career, creating a buzz anytime their teams met.

"Come on, Probie, give me a chance at the title."
- Tie Domi

Probert, who began his career as the enforcer of the Detroit Red Wings, was a few years ahead of Domi and already had the reputation of being the toughest player in the NHL. At 6-foot-3, 225 pounds, it wasn't too hard to figure out why.

Domi, on the other hand, was generously listed at 5-foot-10, but at 207 pounds, he was built like a fire hydrant. As a member of the New York Rangers, 'The Albanian Assassin' wanted a piece of Probert to show the hockey world what he was made of. On Feb. 9, 1992, the two collided.

"Tie was just a young kid coming up and he said 'Come on, Probie, give me a chance at the title,' " Probert recalled in one of his final interviews before passing away in 2010. "And I obliged, because that's how I was brought up in the game."

The match featured big blows from both sides, but a flurry of lefts by Domi late in the scrap seemed to give him the edge. As he was being led away to the penalty box, Domi pantomimed a championship belt being fitted around his waist, crowning himself the new heavyweight champ in the process.

Probert was not amused.

"It's just something you don't do," he said, adding that he made note of the gesture. "You put it in your memory bank."

In the rematch, nearly a year later, Probert challenged Domi just 37 seconds into the first period. This time, the big Red Wing got the upper hand early, crashing down on Domi with a barrage of right hands for a good 20 seconds before Domi could stabilize himself.

"According to Steve (Yzerman), I won the rematch," Probert said.

Between 1992 and 1998, the two fought nine times, including three bouts in '96 when Probert was skating for the Chicago Blackhawks and Domi was a member of the Toronto Maple Leafs.

"He reminded me of Stan Jonathan; low center of gravity, pretty stocky guy," Probert noted. "He'd try to get you in tight and land those big haymakers."

And while Probert and Domi looked like they were out for blood on the ice, enforcers never took it personally back then. In fact, in the days before charter plane flights, teams often stayed in opposing cities overnight, meaning run-ins in public often occurred.

"I remember fighting Bob McGill one night, then seeing him at a bar after the game," Probert said. "It's not even brought up. There was the code that you left it on the ice."

The two even crossed paths in another pastime as contestants on the CBC figure skating reality show *Battle of the Blades* in 2009.

"He's actually a pretty good guy," Probert chuckled. "We just laugh about the old times. There's no hard feelings."

MONTREAL CANADIENS
TORONTO MAPLE LEAFS

It has been said that people who live in Montreal can't wait for Friday night, while people who live in Toronto can't wait until Monday morning.

The idea is that there exists more of a *joie de vivre* in Montreal, which is only logical since it is a French expression. That, and it's kind of true. Toronto has been, and will always be, the buttoned-down business hub of Canada. Montreal, on the other hand, is where attractive people dress well and take themselves a little less seriously.

When it comes to hockey, you can see why the people of Montreal have had just a little more spring in their steps over, say, the past 40 years or so.

The two most storied Canadian teams in hockey, Toronto and Montreal, always get up for each other.

Since expansion, the Canadiens have essentially taken the Maple Leafs out to the woodshed in just about every category imaginable. The rivalry between Canada's two biggest cities still runs deep, but that is based more on long-ago clashes rather than those in the modern day.

The two teams haven't even met in the playoffs since 1979, for heaven's sake, but that doesn't stop fans of the two teams for having a pretty good hate-on for one another. Over the past 20 years or so, the two franchises can't seem to get it right when it comes to being good at the same time, but even when it's a meaningless game in March, there's an electricity in the air all day when the Maple Leafs are in Montreal that you don't see at any other time.

First of all, Maple Leaf fans invade Montreal. They swarm the streets by day, they take over Schwartz's Deli at lunchtime, they cheer from the cheap seats during the games and hit the bars afterward. Imagine what would happen if these two teams ever met in a Stanley Cup final, something that hasn't happened since the Leafs beat the Canadiens in 1967.

Since then, though, it's been a Montreal rout. The Canadiens have won 10 Stanley Cups since the Leafs last won it. In terms of individual awards, the Canadiens have won 90 of them in their history, compared to just 34 for the Maple Leafs (Can you believe the Leafs have never had a Norris Trophy winner? Montreal has had 11 of them.) The Canadiens have had 16 MVPs in their history, the Maple Leafs two. Montreal has had 28 Vezinas, the Leafs six. The Leafs do have a commanding lead 9-2 in Lady Byng Trophies, which really isn't something about which you go around beating your chest.

But it wasn't always this way. Prior to expansion, the Maple Leafs and Candiens were fierce rivals. When the Maple Leafs defeated the Canadiens in '67, the Canadiens were two-time winners prior to that and won the next two, meaning that had they won in '67, they would have won five in a row. It was also the year Montreal was hosting the World's Fair and if you ask any old-time Canadiens about that loss, they'll admit it still sticks in their craws.

"He nearly bit my finger off." – Butch Bouchard

"The Toronto Maple leafs are becoming almost as proficient at winning Stanley Cups as the Montreal Canadiens," The Hockey News said after the Leafs won their 11th Stanley Cup in '67.

But the rivalry goes way, way back and takes its roots in 1946 when Frank Selke left the Leafs to rebuild the Canadiens. Selke had been the Maple Leafs' assistant GM under Conn Smythe, but when Smythe went off to fight in the second World War, he returned to find what he perceived as an attempt by Selke to take his job. The fact that Selke traded Frank Eddolls to the Canadiens for the rights to Ted Kennedy without his approval set Smythe off.

"Eddolls had joined the Air Force soon after signing with us," Smythe later wrote in his book *If You Can't Beat 'Em in the Alley*, "and I thought trading him was a stinking trick to play on a man who was going overseas."

Forget that Kennedy went down as one of the greatest players in Leaf franchise history while Eddolls had an undistinguished career in parts of three seasons with the Canadiens. Selke was sent packing and went about building the Canadiens into a powerhouse.

And there were ugly incidents to be sure. In January, 1949, Ken Reardon of the Canadiens and Cal Gardner of the Leafs got involved in a stick swinging duel that THN described as, "nothing short of barbaric."

Gardner broke his stick over Reardon's back and Reardon retaliated. Then he went at Gardner and broke his jaw with a punch. Two years later, Reardon was contrite about the incident and said, "I'm going to walk into the Leafs dressing room and shake hands with Gardner."

To which Gardner replied, "He might as well stay out for all the good it will do him." When asked whether that might be a callous attitude, he snorted, "Like hell. Who did all the suffering?"

Another ugly incident occurred in the 1951-52 season when Rocket Richard and Bill Juzda became involved in a fight that resulted in Richard one-punching Juzda, who fell to the ice face-first with his arms crossed in front of him. Richard and Fern Flaman were involved in an altercation and Juzda intervened. As the two were skating off the ice, Richard drilled Juzda.

"If Juzda had minded his own business then nothing would have happened to him," Richard told THN. "Flaman and I were fighting, it had nothing to do with him. It'll teach him to mind his own business from now on."

"I thought trading him was a stinking trick."
- Conn Smythe

"(Richard) has never hit another player when he was looking," Juzda told THN, "but geez, how he can punch."

Earlier in the altercation, Canadiens captain Emile 'Butch' Bouchard and Juzda were also going at it. "He nearly bit my finger off," Bouchard told THN. "I'm going to ask President (Clarence) Campbell if he will order that guy to wear a muzzle the next time."

Things are a bit more civil now between the cities that represent Canada's two solitudes. Heck, Canadiens fans were even belting out the Canadian national anthem in *English* during the 2010 playoffs. But that comportment will likely go out the window if these two teams can ever find a way to get back to the Stanley Cup final again.

Oh yeah, and the Leafs can take solace in the fact that, when everything is on the line, they still lead the Canadiens 3-2 in head-to-head Stanley Cup finals.

MIKE MILBURY
THE WORLD

Beer or brouhaha; those were Mike Milbury's options.

He was in the visitors dressing room in Madison Square Garden, gearing down and thinking about his Christmas holidays following the conclusion of a game between his Boston Bruins and the New York Rangers when he noticed a serious dearth of teammates around, save for goalie Gerry Cheevers.

Turns out the rest of the Bruins were busy chasing Rangers fans through the stands after one spectator, a 30-year-old man named John Kaptain, allegedly leaned over the glass during an altercation after the final buzzer and whacked Bruins tough guy Stan Jonathan with a program before making off with his stick.

As a coach, player, GM and analyst, Mike Milbury has left his irreverent mark on the hockey world.

Led by Terry O'Reilly, who believed Kaptain had punched Jonathan, the Bruins tore into the stands in search of revenge. Word eventually reached Milbury in the dressing room and he had to make a call; stay and have a social drink with the goalie or beat up some Blueshirts backers.

"I was already on my second beer," Cheevers, who was going nowhere, told the New York *Times* with a laugh when recalling the night's events 30 years after the fact.

Milbury was a little more motivated by the opportunity to enter the fray and the night of mayhem remains an infamous one thanks to the vision of Milbury whacking Kaptain with his own shoe after he'd been cornered by the trio of Milbury, O'Reilly and the normally more reserved Peter McNab.

> **"Everybody was focusing on the idiot highest up in the stands hitting somebody with a shoe."**
> **- Mike Milbury**

Those were just three of 18 Boston players who got up close and personal with New York fans that evening, but it's that image of Milbury giving Kaptain some tough loafer love that lives on.

"If you watch the tape – and I can freely throw my teammates under the bus now 30 years later – people were throwing some serious shots down below us that were obscured by the fact that everybody was focusing on the idiot highest up in the stands hitting somebody with a shoe," Milbury told the *Times*.

Milbury and McNab were given six-game suspensions by NHL president John Ziegler, while O'Reilly drew an eight-game sentence. All three were fined $500.

Kaptain, who has since passed away, launched a lawsuit in 1980 that never amounted to much. But that doesn't mean Milbury is short on battles to fight. From hurling insults at player agents to tearing a strip of those people he feels are for the 'pansification' hockey, the hard-hitting former defenseman, coach, GM and current TV analyst is never short on opinions.

During his decade-long tenure as GM of the New York Islanders from the mid-1990s through 2006, Milbury had a somewhat acrimonious round of contract negotiations with sniper Ziggy Palffy. When commenting on Palffy's agent, Paul Kraus, a frustrated Milbury offered up this timeless gem:

"It's too bad he lives in the city. He's depriving some small village of a pretty good idiot."

Anybody who saw Milbury log huge penalty minutes on the Bruins blueline from 1976 through 1987, or barking at players and fellow coaches as Boston's bench boss for two seasons in the early 1990s, knows he takes an old-school approach to the game. That's why it was no surprise Milbury invented a word – 'pansification' – to describe what he thought some people were trying to do the game when discussing things like whether fighting has a place in hockey as an analyst on *Hockey Night in Canada*.

The term actually drew the ire of a group called Equality for Gays and Lesbians Everywhere, which filed a complaint with the CBC's ombudsman.

There was also the famous tale of Milbury supposedly driving former Isles goalie Tommy Salo to tears during an arbitration hearing back in the late '90s, but, years later, Milbury claimed it was a false story drummed up by Salo's agent in order to gather sympathy for his client.

Milbury declined comment for this story, but his CBC co-worker, Kelly Hrudey, confirmed that the version of Milbury people see on their TV isn't a whole lot different than his real-life persona.

"How he behaves on air is exactly who he is away from the studio and I think that's what makes him really endearing or popular because he's not putting on an act," said Hrudey, adding if there is a difference, it's that Milbury is a little less gruff when the cameras aren't rolling.

Hrudey was just coming into the league when Milbury was on his way out. Still, the old Isles and Los Angeles Kings goalie was very aware the scrappy Massachusetts boy had a well-earned reputation for tough play and a willingness to follow through on menacing promises.

"He really backed it up. That's the thing that stood out to me," Hrudey said. "He didn't talk a great game, then go out and just play like everybody else. He was a physical force out there, for sure."

Milbury is rarely shy about offering up his take, but one area in which he may be a bit tight-lipped is when offering insight into the real impetus behind some of the bad trades he made while at the helm of the Isles. He is most frequently skewered for the deal that sent Olli Jokinen and Roberto Luongo to Florida in 2000, clearing the way for the Isles to draft

Rick DiPietro first overall in 2000, and the swap that sent a young Zdeno Chara and the second overall selection in the 2001 draft to Ottawa – which used the pick to take Jason Spezza – in return for enigmatic Russian Alexei Yashin.

It's easy to pile the blame on Milbury for those moves and while some bad decisions were certainly completely his own error in judgment, he also toiled under some extremely volatile, meddlesome and even criminal ownership groups on Long Island.

"He took all the shots and he's a good guy, he gets kidded all the time on TV and radio and in the papers as 'Mad Mike,' but he didn't make all those trades," said Don Cherry, Milbury's colleague at the CBC and his former coach in Boston.

Added Hrudey: "There will always be mistakes on (a GM's) record. It's just the nature of the business. Secondly, just because you are a manager doesn't mean you're calling all the shots."

As for how malleable Milbury can be, Hrudey said beyond the bluster is a man who can keep an open mind to other points of view.

"He does have those old-school values, but he certainly has no problem engaging people in a conversation if they see it another way," Hrudey noted. "If you actually have enough points to back up what you're trying to say, he is very much willing to listen and take note of it."

VS. ERIC LINDROS
BOBBY CLARKE

On paper, it promised to be a perfect relationship, with one Hall of Fame hockey icon getting the chance to work with someone many thought to be a certain future inductee.

But although relations between Flyers GM Bob Clarke and Eric Lindros started off OK, it took only a few years before the association began to show cracks.

After a mega-trade from Quebec to the Flyers in 1992, Lindros started to bring Philadelphia back to respectability and won his first and only MVP in the strike-shortened 1994-95 campaign, when the Flyers ended a five-year playoff drought.

Soon after, injuries began to plague Lindros, headlined by a series of concussions that unofficially originated in a game where Pittsburgh defenseman Darius Kasparaitis leveled him with a check just after the 1998 Winter Olympics.

However, the injury that really drove a wedge between Clarke and Lindros occurred on April 1, 1999 when the 'Big E' sustained a collapsed lung due to a tear from a hit by Nashville defenseman Bob Boughner.

According to Clarke, Lindros' parents, Carl and Bonnie, later accused the GM of allowing their son to fly back to Philadelphia after his release from a Nashville hospital, a risky proposition due to changes in cabin pressure.

"Eric brings all the problems on himself," Clarke said at the time. "It's pretty hard to believe (our training staff) wouldn't treat him properly, or (that) I'd put him on a plane to try to kill him.

"This kind of stuff never ends and it's hard on a club. It's disruptive. You can't tell me a 27-year-old man could have his dad speaking for him, taking him to the doctor, showing up in the locker room after an injury. You do that to a 14-year-old boy and he's embarrassed."

Bobby Clarke brought his hard-nosed style on the ice to his battles with Eric Lindros once Clarke became GM of the Flyers.

Lindros survived but the problems continued. Over his nine years with the Flyers, he sustained an estimated six concussions, the last and most famous one in 2000 that completely ended his relationship with Clarke and the Flyers.

> **"I've got nothing but good things to take away from what occurred as far as the players and fans. That certainly overrides anything that took place with management."**
> **– Eric Lindros**

In Game 7 of the 2000 Eastern Conference final, Lindros was knocked unconscious on a highlight reel hit by New Jersey's Scott Stevens. The Devils completed a three-game comeback with a win in that contest and Lindros was on his way out the door.

"Over the years, I think there were way too many controversies," Clarke said before trading Lindros to the Rangers on Aug. 20, 2001 for Jan Hlavac, Kim Johnsson, Pavel Brendl and a third round draft pick. "He gets hit (by Stevens) and his dad and his butler are running around the locker room."

Lindros never really had pointed public criticism for Clarke. Instead, he just referred to the difficulty in the abstract.

"There was a tremendous amount of support in Philadelphia," Lindros said at his introductory press conference with the Rangers. "Come play-off time, that city was rocking.

"Even through the many highs and lows, there was always support. I've got nothing but good things to take away from what occurred as far as the players and fans. That certainly overrides anything that took place with management."

TED LINDSAY
THE NHL

VS.

The fact the current crop of NHL players decided to rename the trophy awarded to their MVP after him says all that needs to be said about the reverence reserved for Ted Lindsay.

But 'Terrible' Ted lived up to his nickname (based on his rugged on-ice play) when he took on the NHL establishment and sought justice for the players way back in 1956-57, when owners treated NHLers like serfs, setting into motion the founding of the NHL Players' Association in the process.

"I did it because I believed in it," Lindsay said. "The owners met 10 times a year; we never met."

Hall of Famer Ted Lindsay went to war for players' rights.

Back in the Original Six era, players on opposing teams barely tolerated each other and fraternizing was out of the question. The only reprieve came during the All-Star Game, which back then was played before the regular season began.

Lindsay and Montreal defenseman Doug Harvey led the charge, speaking through team captains and eventually collecting $100 from every player in the NHL except one – Ted 'Teeder' Kennedy of the Toronto Maple Leafs.

"He didn't believe in it and I have no problem with that," Lindsay recalled. "I hated his guts when I played against him, but he was a hell of a player and I respected him."

The players had enlisted the help of two New York City lawyers, Norman Lewis and Milton Mound, who had worked with Major League Baseball players in their union efforts and were introduced to Lindsay through Cleveland Indians pitcher Bob Feller.

"Adams was a jerk. Dumbest manager in all of hockey."
- Ted Lindsay

On the surface, the powers that be in the NHL had no idea what was going on. The season proceeded without a peep until February, when the players were ready to make their union known. On a Monday night (traditionally a travel day when no games were scheduled), the players held a press conference at 3 p.m. to ensure the wire services had time to blast out the announcement. Owners, GMs, even coaches had no idea what was coming.

"Believe me," Lindsay said, "that hurt them more than anything else."

Ironically, Lindsay believes the one player who was hurt most by the secret union movement was Teeder Kennedy – because he didn't tell Maple Leafs owner Conn Smythe what was happening.

"Smythe had come back from the (Second World) War and he believed in loyalty," Lindsay said. "I believe it cost Kennedy a lifetime job with the Leafs because he kept our secret."

Not surprisingly, Lindsay was also targeted by the enraged NHL owners. Despite finishing second in league scoring to linemate Gordie Howe in '56-57, Lindsay was shipped off to the woeful Chicago Black Hawks that summer along with Glenn Hall in exchange for Johnny Wilson, Forbes Kennedy, Hank Bassen and Bill Preston. The triggerman on the deal was GM Jack Adams, the powerful and intimidating muscle for Detroit owner James Norris. Adams would often bench or demote players to the minors on the slightest whim; he was the living embodiment of why the players wanted a union in the first place.

"Adams was a jerk," Lindsay said. "Dumbest manager in all of hockey – and I say that in all honesty."

Back then, however, Adams had the ear of the press and never missed a chance to slam his former star once Lindsay was traded.

"I can tell you, Howe won't miss Lindsay a bit," Adams told THN before the 1957-58 season. He helped Lindsay more than Lindsay helped him." For the record, Howe's production dipped for several years after Lindsay became a Hawk. But what Adams got wrong in prognostication, he made up for in witty propaganda.

"Only one thing hurt me as Lindsay went into the dictionary to denounce me," Adams said. "That was his statement I had made uncomplimentary remarks about his wife.

"I never met his wife. So far as I know, she is a most admirable woman. She must be, to put up with Lindsay."

Adams also had the benefit of a cozy relationship with the press. When he wasn't cutting down Lindsay, he got the media to do the sniping for him. Lindsay's salary – generally in the high four figures back then – was reported instead to be at least $20,000, while unnamed Red Wings were quoted as saying they were glad Lindsay was gone. Of course, the reporter hadn't *asked* the unnamed source – Adams had fed him the quote second-hand.

Needless to say, the two never made up.

"There was no apology expected, no apology necessary," Lindsay added. "He had a job to do and I was doing what I thought was right." Even though the initial union movement lost steam in 1958, the seeds

> **"I never met his wife. So far as I know, she is a most admirable woman. She must be, to put up with Lindsay."**
> **- Jack Adams**

planted by Lindsay and Harvey had begun to slowly take root and by 1967, agent Alan Eagleson helped found the NHL Players' Association. In 2010, what was the Lester B. Pearson Award – the league's MVP as voted on by the players – was renamed the Ted Lindsay Award in honor of the man's service to his profession. To this day, Lindsay is steadfast in his beliefs.

"Edmonton was our farm club in the Western League, Indianapolis in the American League," Lindsay said of his days with the Wings. "I'm making $5,500. The guys in Edmonton or Indianapolis are on two-way contracts and I saw things happen to these kids...(Adams) would send kids to Edmonton, wouldn't pay them five cents. 'You're gone, kid.' It was a dictatorship.

"I wanted the owners to know I was not stupid. I had brains."

VS. BOSTON BRUINS
MONTREAL CANADIENS

In Don Cherry's defense, he was only answering the question asked of him.

It was during the classic 1979 Stanley Cup semifinal series between the Boston Bruins and Montreal Canadiens that Cherry, one of Canada's most outspoken supporters, experienced a little trouble getting into his home country from the United States.

The Bruins had just scored a massive 5-2 Game 6 win over the Habs in the Garden to force a decisive Game 7 in Montreal. Waiting in the final were the overachieving New York Rangers, a team widely considered to be fodder for either the three-time defending-champion Canadiens or the powerhouse Bruins.

Cherry was asked a very standard question while passing through customs, but his reply was far from stock.

"You know how they ask, 'What's your purpose for coming to Canada?' " Cherry relayed. "I said, 'To beat the f---in' Montreal Canadiens.' "

The Bruins bench boss may have just been speaking from the heart, but his stated agenda didn't go over very well with the customs agents who immediately flagged him as a potential threat to national hockey security.

"Every bag of mine was all over the place, (even) my shaving kits," he said, noting every piece of his luggage was picked over before he was finally allowed to proceed.

Once they got to Montreal, Cherry and his Bruins nearly did knock off the vaunted Habs, but an untimely too-many-men-on-the-ice penalty was their undoing, as Guy Lafleur tied the score 4-4 late in the third. Yvon Lambert tallied in overtime for the Habs to add another legendary chapter to the long rivalry between the two teams.

Every inch of ice was contested when the Habs and Bruins squared off in the 1970s, as it still is today.

Montreal went on to beat the Rangers and claim its fourth consecutive Cup. The previous two years they had beaten Boston in the final with a club many consider to be the best ever assembled. And it had to be, because the Bruins were a lethal combination of skill and toughness in the late 1970s, a time when the feud with Montreal likely reached its zenith because both sides iced legitimate Cup-contending clubs every year.

In addition to snipers such as Lafleur and Steve Shutt, the Habs also benefited greatly from 'The Big Three' blueline trio of Larry Robinson, Serge Savard and Guy Lapointe.

"They were so powerful and had such depth, that you get in a seven-game series with them, it was impossible to win because they had Robinson, Savard and Lapointe on all the time," Cherry said. "You walk into (The Forum), it was like going into the lion's den."

Historically, Montreal has dominated the playoff rivalry between the teams, though Boston has had its moments. The most amazing run of Habs supremacy stretched all the way from 1946 to 1987, when the Canadiens won an unbelievable 18 consecutive playoff series over Boston, prompting many to suggest the B's were simply incapable of victory when it came to facing Montreal in the post-season.

> ## "It was like going into the lion's den."
> ## - Don Cherry

But that theory was eviscerated when a determined bunch of Bruins finally bested the Habs in a five-game series in 1988 after having lost to Montreal the previous four years in the playoffs.

"It's over," long-suffering Bruin Keith Crowder told The Hockey News at the time. "The jinx is dead. What jinx? What hex? What Forum? All kaput."

And it was, mostly. Though they never were able to bring a title to Boston, the Bruins teams led by the likes of Ray Bourque, Cam Neely and Andy Moog had their way with the Habs, winning five of six playoff series between '88 and 1994.

Most recently, the Canadiens have been able regain the upper hand, winning three of four series between the teams in the 2000s to run their all-time playoff series record against their southern rivals to 24-8.

Of those 24 triumphs, the most notable include the aforementioned '79 series, the massive Ken Dryden-led upset of the heavily-favored Bruins in 1971 and the series that may have given hockey it's best picture ever, the 1952 Stanley Cup semifinal clash.

It was in the seventh game of that showdown that Maurice Richard, bleeding over the eye and still woozy from a second-period collision with Boston right winger Leo Labine, scored a spectacular goal late in the third to give Montreal the lead in a game it eventually won 3-1.

After the contest, photographer Roger St. Jean captured one of the game's more enduring images as Bruins goalie 'Sugar' Jim Henry, himself sporting a black eye, seems to almost bow to the Rocket as the two men shake hands while blood trickles down Richard's cheek.

When asked what happened on the collision with Labine, Richard answered very honestly.

"I don't know," he told The Hockey News. "Suddenly, everything went black and the next thing I knew I woke up in the medical room. And I want to tell you, I was still groggy when I scored that goal. I don't remember it clearly."

Boston coach Lynn Patrick didn't have any trouble recalling it.

"I have never seen a better goal," he told THN. "When he saw his chance and cut for the net he looked like only one thing, a rocket. That's how he got the name, and it fits."

Steve Begin is in a unique position to speak about the conflict between Montreal and Boston, having spent four-plus seasons with the Habs beginning in 2003-04, before signing with the B's for the 2009-10 campaign.

Like all great hockey feuds, the feelings of hate extend well beyond the boys on the ice, spilling into stands where backers of the black and gold and the bleu, blanc et rouge do whatever they can to give their beloved squads an advantage.

"I've seen both sides and it's funny how each team hates each other, especially the fans," Begin said. "But it's fun. I'm glad I've been on both sides.

"At playoff time it's always one or two notches higher, but it was fun. It's a lot of intensity on the ice and in the stands."

> "I've seen both sides and it's funny how each team hates each other, especially the fans."
> - Steve Begin

VS. WAYNE GRETZKY
NEW JERSEY

It's hard enough to lose. Harder, even, when the score is lopsided. And harder again when the greatest player in the game rubs salt in your wounds. But that's what happened Nov. 19, 1983 when the New Jersey Devils visited the Edmonton Oilers.

The '83-84 season wasn't exactly a banner one for the Devils. Two years removed from a move out of Colorado and coming off a 17-win season, the Devils were just trying to make some headway in the Garden State.

When New Jersey limped into Edmonton to play the juggernaut Oilers, the Devils did so with a record of 2-17-0. After a 13-4 drubbing, Wayne Gretzky ripped the Devils right to their core, calling the franchise a "Mickey Mouse operation" that was ruining hockey.

Ouch.

> "He was young at the time and I'm sure he didn't expect it to have the repercussions it did."
> - Marshall Johnston

"I happened to be coaching that game," said Marshall Johnston an assistant coach with the Devils under Billy MacMillan in early 1983. "It was into the third period and we got a penalty. Out come Wayne and (Jari) Kurri and (Paul) Coffey and (Glenn) Anderson...and then, of course, after the game there was the comment."

So Gretzky – who had three goals and eight points on the night – and the Oilers weren't exactly taking it easy on the Devils, on the ice or off.

There was more depth to Gretzky's comment, but it was "Mickey Mouse operation" that made hockey headlines. It didn't matter what he meant or didn't mean, that characterization was all anyone cared about.

"He was young at the time and I'm sure he didn't expect it to have the repercussions it did," Johnston said. "But it did."

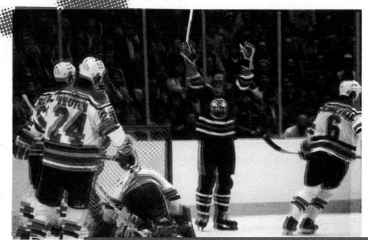
Wayne Gretzky made headlines when he slammed the hapless New Jersey Devils.

Three days after the Gretzky comment, Devils owner John McMullen cleaned house, firing coach-GM MacMillan and player personnel director Bert Marshall. Johnston was moved upstairs from behind the bench to become the team's director of player personnel.

"The owner was embarrassed," Johnston said, "as we all were."

Gretzky later clarified his statement, taking a long view.

"(The Devils) are going to lose a lot of games," he said. "They're going to have an empty building soon and we're going to be without another team. I hope for the league's sake the Devils turn it around."

Well they didn't – at least not that season, finishing with a 17-56-7 record, good for second-last overall. (To add insult to injury, by finishing with three more points than Pittsburgh, New Jersey missed a chance to draft a Quebec junior named Mario Lemieux.)

"We were struggling as it was and there were a lot of games where we felt embarrassed," Johnston said when asked if there was any pushback from Devils players against Gretzky later in the year. "Everyone would try to do their best and it wasn't good enough. That was the bottom line. That's what happened."

If the Devils players wouldn't or couldn't push back, what Devils fans there were did, in a manner of speaking. When the Oilers next made their way to East Rutherford, New Jersey supporters were there – with Mickey Mouse masks on.

VS. DANY HEATLEY
OTTAWA SENATORS

Dany Heatley's move to the Ottawa Senators was born from tragedy. In fall 2003, Heatley, driving with teammate Dan Snyder, lost control of his speeding Ferrari 360 Modena. Heatley was severely injured, and Snyder died six days after the crash. After two years of rehab and toiling away in Atlanta, Heatley asked for a trade amid rumors that he wanted a change of scenery to put the unspeakable incident behind him.

Dany Heatley's trade request was not taken well by fans of the Ottawa Senators.

On Aug. 23, 2005, Heatley's wish was granted. The Thrashers sent him to the Ottawa Senators in exchange for superstar winger Marian Hossa and veteran defenseman Greg de Vries. Heatley's arrival immediately formed one of the most dangerous lines in hockey, the "CASH Line" (Captain Daniel Alfredsson, Jason Spezza and Heatley).

Heatley, a superstar in his own right, came into the fold already with a 41-goal, 89-point season under his belt, so needless to say there were some expectations for him to perform, especially with such talented line mates. Heatley did not disappoint. Over the next two seasons, Heatley turned in back-to-back 50-goal, 100-plus-point seasons, culminating with a 2007 run to the Stanley Cup final. The Senators were dispatched in five games by the Anaheim Ducks but Heatley had come in and made the "CASH Line" the top performing line in hockey and a force to be reckoned with.

"I was shocked and disappointed," – Bryan Murray

Following the Cup loss, Heatley re-upped with the Senators to the tune of a six-year contract extension worth $45 million. That season, Heatley managed to score 41 goals and 82 points despite missing 11 games with a separated shoulder. The following season however, Heatley and the rest of the "CASH Line" suffered a departure from their recent successes, point production and seeding in the standings, costing coach Craig Hartsburg his job.

Cory Clouston, coach of the Senators' farm team in Binghamton was brought in to fill the void left by Hartsburg. Clouston brought a new system to the table, one that would result in diminished ice-time and a move to the second power play unit for Heatley. Heatley finished the season with his lowest point totals since his rookie season.

On June 10, 2009, it was reported that Heatley had requested a trade. Citing an unhappiness with his role under Clouston, Heatley thought it would be best to move on elsewhere. This levelled the Senators and their fans. "I was shocked and disappointed," said Senators GM Brian Murray at a press conference. "The frustrating part for us is we have gone through several coaches here that we couldn't win enough games with. We brought in a guy, the results we were very happy with. The team started to look like a real team again. And then to be kind of blindsided in his way of thinking anyway by one of your players – not wanting to fit in – that's hard for a coach to accept."

The Senators then took on the unenviable task of trading a superstar who had made his demands public. On June 30, 2009 – two days before the Senators were on the hook to pay Heatley a $4 million bonus – a trade was reached with the Edmonton Oilers to send Heatley in exchange for Andrew Cogliano, Dustin Penner and Ladislav Smid. Heatley – whose contract held a no-trade clause – refused the trade, furthering the boiling resentment towards the star winger in the nation's capital.

After a summer of can-kicking and posturing, the Senators were finally able to reach a deal with the San Jose Sharks. Heatley was sent along with a fifth round pick to the Sharks in return for Milan Michalek, Jonathan Cheechoo and a second round pick.

"The team started to look like a real team again."
– Murray

Heatley's antics were not quickly forgotten. Demanding a trade has always been an unpopular decision amongst Canadian hockey fans and they let him hear it nationwide while playing with the Sharks, primarily in Edmonton and Ottawa. Heatley's participation with the 2010 Canadian Olympic gold medal winning team did wonders to smooth his reputation with the rest of Canada, but in Ottawa Dany Heatley will remain one of the most hated players of all time.

VS. KINGSTON FRONTENACS
BELLEVILLE BULLS

Less than an hour apart by car, the small, eastern Ontario cities of Kingston and Belleville have had a running feud for as long as anyone can remember. Other than geography, the reasons for the rivalry differ depending on who you ask, but one thing everyone can agree on is that sports have always been a focal point. And the Ontario League's Kingston Frontenacs and Belleville Bulls carry the banner of biggest game in town for both lo cales.

Craig Mills played with Belleville from 1993 to 1996, captaining the team his final two seasons.

"It was pretty clear right off the hop my first season," he said. "The vets made it clear that Kingston is the team we love to hate and we hate to lose to. Before even one exhibition game I knew the rivalry was an intense one.

"And they hated us as much as we hated them. It was definitely one of the best rivalries I had in my career."

Larry Mavety knows just what that's all about. He's been a part of the Bulls-Fronts rivalry since the beginning and part of the civic rivalry even longer; his family moved to Belleville when he was 12 years old.

"I think it's been the same here forever," Mavety said. "I played baseball against Kingston and, way back when, Jr. B hockey, and back in the old senior hockey days it was a Belleville-Kingston rivalry, too. We used to have fights in ball.

"It just seems it's something that's been built here over the years going back quite a way."

The Bulls joined the Frontenacs in the OHL for the 1981-82 season with Mavety behind the bench. Twenty-nine years on and the journeyman pro – he was a rugged defenseman with some offensive punch who played nearly 250 World Hockey Association games – hasn't had a job outside of hockey or an office outside of Belleville; unless it was in Kingston, which it is now.

Nothing goes according to plan when Belleville and Kingston mix it up in the Ontario League.

From 1981 to 1988, he coached the Bulls, then left town to become Kingston's coach. Two years later, he was back in Belleville for another seven-year stint behind the bench. Then it was back to the Frontenacs for six seasons ending in 2003. He then moved upstairs to become Kingston's full-time GM.

"When I was in Belleville I wanted to beat Kingston and when I was here I wanted to beat Belleville," said the bombastic Mavety, known for his pre-game rants and his signature move: kicking the dressing room door on his way out. "Even though I started in Belleville and everything else, when I came here it just switched.

"I hated them when I was coaching…the players wouldn't know how much I wanted to beat Belleville when I was coaching in Kingston and vice versa."

Frustrating Fronts fans for decades is the fact the Bulls almost always seem to get the better of Kingston, including a 12-8 win in the teams' first-ever contest. And through the years, Mavety has learned no lead is ever safe.

"It's just been something that's one of those things," Mavety said. "It doesn't matter how good Belleville is or how good Kingston is, the games were always close and then Belleville for some reason (wins)…I have no idea why."

Belleville has won five division titles since entering the league, Kingston has just one in that time. Belleville has finished with more points than Kingston 20 times, the Frontenacs have bested the Bulls eight times – the two teams also finished one season tied. Along the way, Belleville has finished last in the division three times; Kingston on 12 occasions. And the Bulls have lost just one of six playoff series to the Frontenacs.

Close scores, crazy games and having the same coach bounce back and forth between the two teams play into it, but rivalries are made in the playoffs. The old-school Mavety has tasted both the agony of defeat and the sweetness of victory, from both benches.

> **"Kingston is the team we love to hate and we hate to lose to."**
> **– Craig Mills**

In 1989, Mavety's Frontenacs finished just a point out of first overall in the entire league. Mavety was the OHL's coach of the year and two of his players made post-season all-star teams. Eric Lindros' Oshawa Generals finished atop the league, but the Fronts had a winning record against them that season. Things were setting up nicely for a long play-off run.

Problem was, the Frontenacs ran into the Bulls in the first round. Seven games later – including a six-hour, 16-minute, four-overtime marathon (the longest game in league history) – Belleville prevailed. And that after Belleville's first-team all-star goaltender Jeff Fife was given a 10-game suspension for throwing his stick into the crowd at the Kingston Memorial Arena. The Bulls called up a Jr. B goalie who won three of the next four games to take the series, stopping 115 shots in the victories.

Kingston was crushed. Oshawa played for the Memorial Cup.

"That was a hell of a hockey club, it should really have gone on," Mavety said. "Probably my biggest disappointment in hockey was that year."

In 1994-95, the script was flipped for the coach. Just not for Kingston.

The Frontenacs won their first and only division title, finishing 20 points ahead of Belleville in the standings. Led by David Ling, the national player of the year after a 61-goal, 135-point season that included 136 penalty minutes in 62 games, third team all-CHL goaltender Tyler Moss and future NHLers Brett Lindros and Chad Kilger, the Fronts were the heavy favorites when they met the Bulls in the second round of the playoffs.

"If there's ever been anyone who could get an arena going it was David Ling," Mills said. "He could get his own arena going and he could get ours going just as easily."

Favorites or not, the Frontenacs and their murderers' row of forwards went down in six games to the Bulls, bringing the franchise's best season to a screeching halt.

"Ling broke his finger and he could only go about half tilt," Mavety remembered. "It's just things like that; fluke things that happen. When I was in Belleville I enjoyed it, in Kingston I don't.

"A lot of things go, I guess, crazy when the two teams play each other."

That '94-95 season the teams played one another 20 times counting pre-season, regular season and post-season contests.

"You knew how everyone played, you knew what to do to get under everyone's skin," Mills said. "And because you knew them so well you wanted to beat them that much more."

VS. THE NORRIS DIVISION
THE NORRIS DIVISION

John Brophy snapped.

Admittedly, such emotional outbursts were common for the ornery white-haired, battle-scarred coach of the Toronto Maple Leafs. But on the night of Feb. 22, 1988, deep in the bowels of the Met Center in Bloomington, Minn., Brophy unleashed a rant for the ages, one that certainly deserves a spot in the all-time Tirade Hall of Fame.

Minutes after Brophy's Leafs had dropped a 4-2 decision to the division-rival Minnesota North Stars, the Buds' bench boss, still seething at his team's moribund effort, hunted down beat writers Lance Hornby of the Toronto *Sun*, Mark Harding of the Toronto *Star* and Gary Loewen of the *Globe & Mail* in order to unleash his venom.

The rest, as they say, is history.

In the course of ripping his team to reporters, Brophy used the f-bomb a whopping 72 times. Recorded at the time by Hornby, the rant has found its way to the Internet, where it has become one of the most popular items among hockey fans on the web.

"It's a disgrace," Brophy spewed that night. "I'm sick and (bleepin') tired of making excuses for all these (bleepin') guys that's getting paid on this (bleepin') hockey club, blaming it on someone else all the (bleepin') time.

"Who are all these (bleepin') people who drag that (bleepin') uniform through the (bleepin') mud? For Christ's sake, there have been great players play in the thing, and then (they) act like this here. Who are they?"

> **"There's a reason they called it the Chuck Norris Division."**
> **- Wendel Clark**

Tough words. Tough coach. Tough division.

When looking back at the Norris Division, perhaps the poster child for the decade would be Brophy.

Showdowns between players like Chicago's Warren Rychel (left) and St. Louis' Tony Twist were common in the 1980s Norris Division.

During one playoff year, the Leaf coach dressed up in a pinstripe suit and a 1930s-type chapeau, causing marketing geniuses to sell replicas of the hat with the words "Brophy's Boys" on the front.

When decked out in that garb, Brophy resembled a gangster from the Al Capone era.

Welcome to the Norris Division of the 1980s, where fierce rivalries and bitter hatred festered. Against division rivals. Against the officials. And, in Brophy's case, sometimes against his own team.

Indeed, whenever the Leafs, North Stars, Chicago Blackhawks, St. Louis Blues and Detroit Red Wings faced off against each other over that 10-year span, life was never boring. Especially for referees.

While the offensively-gifted New York Islanders and Edmonton Oilers dominated the decade thanks to the likes of superstars Bryan Trottier, Mike Bossy, Denis Potvin, Wayne Gretzky and Mark Messier, the prominent names in the Norris Division often belonged to those whose pugilistic skills sometimes outweighed their puck talents: Bob Probert. Shane Churla. Joey Kocur. Paul Holmgren. Basil McRae. John Kordic. Dwight Schofield. Behn Wilson. Even Wendel Clark. The list goes on and on and on.

"There's a reason they called it the Chuck Norris Division," Clark explained with a laugh. "Some of the other divisions were known for their fast skaters and offensive flair. But in the Chuck Norris Division, you had to be ready to play physical every night."

Even if that meant dropping the gloves with family members.

Clark remembers a particular night during his rookie season of 1985-86 when that very thing happened. It was a game between his Leafs and the Red Wings, who featured Barry Melrose – Wendel's cousin – and Joey Kocur, related to Clark through a family marriage.

"It's the last bench-clearing brawl I can recollect, and it started when I hit Barry behind the net," Clark said. "Soon Joey was part of it too. I mean, three guys from Kelvington, Saskatchewan – who would have thought?"

Part of that same brouhaha involved a scrap between Probert and the Leafs' Bob McGill.

"We must have fought for five minutes before Probert head-butted me," McGill said. "He got suspended seven games for that.

"I think I must have fought Probert six times. He was the toughest guy to go up against. He was so much bigger than me. I doubt there has ever been a better 1-2 punch in terms of fighters on the same team than Bob Probert and Joey Kocur."

Having played for both the Leafs and the Hawks during the 1980s, McGill experienced first-hand just how rugged the Chuck Norris Division was.

> ## "It made for some sleepless times before games."
> ## - Bob McGill

"Every team in the division was your bitter rival – none more than another," McGill said. "Every night you knew you were in for a dust-up or two. It made for some sleepless times before games."

One of McGill's lasting memories involves a huge fracas at the end of a game between his Leafs and the Blues at Maple Leaf Gardens early in 1984. At one point, Schofield pulled his Blues jersey off and started skating around the ice waving his arms, causing McGill to wing his helmet at the St. Louis tough guy.

"The crowd was going nuts, as if we'd just won the Stanley Cup," McGill chuckled.

McGill wasn't laughing two weeks later when the teams locked horns again, this time in St. Louis.

"It was Valentine's Day and the headline in the St. Louis paper on game day morning blared: 'WELCOME TO THE ST. LOUIS ST. VALENTINE'S DAY MASSACRE,' " McGill said. "It was all because we were in town. Obviously I didn't get much sleep that afternoon."

The bitterness between Norris Division foes extended off the ice as well. In fact, some of the off-ice shenanigans were just as colorful as the on-ice activities.

Having just broken in with the Blues, Doug Gilmour, a checking-line center at the beginning of his career, learned that lesson during one of his first games against the Blackhawks.

"It was at the old St. Louis Arena," Gilmour said. "We're ready to get going and the Chicago coaches haven't come out yet."

The reason? According to Gilmour, a forklift had been parked directly in front of the coach's office, leaving Hawks bench boss Orval Tessier and his staff stuck inside.

Needless to say, the Hawks accused the Blues of foul play.

"They were pissed," Gilmour said.

Then there was volatile Blues GM Ron Caron. The mere mention of his name makes Gilmour chuckle.

Just like John Brophy, Ron Caron could be just as bitter at his own team as he was against Norris Division rivals. And, just like Brophy, he was not shy about letting his own players know about it.

"We had a guy on our team, Jorgen Pettersson, who would drive Caron nuts," Gilmour said. "(Caron) would be sitting in the press box and throw pens down at Jorgen, who would be on the bench. Jorgen wouldn't pay any attention to it, which drove (Caron) even (crazier)."

On the ice. On the bench. In the press box. Was there nowhere in the Chuck Norris Division where a guy could be safe?

According to NHL disciplinarian Colin Campbell, a defenseman with the Red Wings from 1982-85, well, not really.

"There was one particular game in that old barn in St. Louis when Danny Gare and I both got booted out as part of some melee," Campbell said. "On our way to the dressing room, we saw some fans beating up a cop. We had to come to his rescue."

Tough crowds. Tough division.

"That division was as nasty as it could be," Campbell said. "Back at that time, if I was doing the job I have today, I'd be working every night."

VS. RAY EMERY
OTTAWA SENATORS

Drafted in the fourth round, 99th overall in 2001, the tumultuous relationship between Ray Emery and the Ottawa Senators started as innocently as any between a draftee and drafter. After spending the better part of four seasons developing with the Sault Ste. Marie Greyhounds of the Ontario League and the Senators' American League farm team in Binghamton after being drafted, Emery was finally brought up to the big club to fill the backup role behind Dominik Hasek at the start of the 2005-06 season.

High hopes were thrust upon the young goalie by the Senators and their fans after he won the first nine starts of his career. Those high hopes turned to expectations when, after Hasek was injured at the 2006 Olympics, Emery was given the starting job for the remainder of the season. He took the opportunity and ran with it.

"He didn't, in my opinion, commit to the team."
- Bryan Murray

He won 23 games that season and had the Senators primed for a deep playoff run. They ended up bowing out after a hard-fought, five-game second round series with the Buffalo Sabres. But optimism – as always with the Sens goalies – remained the name of game in Ottawa. For the first time in a long time, Emery had given the Senators a reason to be excited about the man tending their twine.

Ray Emery's tumultuous time in Ottawa did include a Stanley Cup final appearance in 2007.

Despite Emery's stellar play the previous season, veteran goalie Martin Gerber was brought in to challenge for the starting job. Although not given the job out of the gate, it didn't take long for Emery to win it back. He put up career-highs in wins, goals-against average and save percentage, leading the Senators to another playoff berth. But late in the season Emery first exhibited the extraordinary and brash personality that would lead to his eventual demise in the Canadian capital.

In a February 2007 game against the Buffalo Sabres, a line brawl erupted early in the second period, as it happens, one of the most peculiar of it's kind. A Chris Neil hit on Sabres captain Chris Drury incited the brouhaha, during which Emery – a trained boxer and avid fan of the sweet science – skated to center ice and taunted the lesser-equipped Sabres goalie Martin Biron into a fight. Biron obliged and, after making quick work of him, Emery was forced to defend himself against Sabres tough guy Andrew Peters; Emery did so grinning like a Cheshire cat. Although wildly entertaining, his actions sparked Senators fans to wonder what to make of the new-found bravado.

Going into the playoffs that season, Emery – now nicknamed "Sugar Ray" – answered his critics, leading the Senators to their first Stanley Cup berth since re-joining the league after a 59-year hiatus. The Sens knocked off Pittsburgh in Round 1, New Jersey in Round 2 and late-season dance partner Buffalo in the conference final, each in five games. Ottawa was set to face Anaheim for the Stanley Cup. Despite Ottawa's best efforts, the Ducks sent the Sens packing in five games. It was after that crushing defeat that the wheels began to fall off for Emery.

The following year, a pre-season injury combined with inspired play from Martin Gerber relegated Emery to back-up duty once again. He took it to heart. A few months into the season Emery's frustration began to show. First with a decline in play, then through reports of inappropriate practice behavior; a lackluster work ethic, fit-throwing and even reported mid-practice fights with teammates Brian McGrattan and Chris Neil surfaced. Emery found himself in trouble with the team on what seemed a weekly basis. The reports spawned trade rumors, ones that refused to go away.

It appeared that Ottawa had soured on Emery; players, fans and personnel alike. And with each sub-standard performance, followed by dressing room altercation, Emery seemed to have soured on them. Just a few months prior he had carried the Sens to the Cup final, now, with the trade deadline looming, a move seemed imminent.

But the deadline came and went and no such deal was reached. A few weeks later, Senators GM Brian Murray admitted that he had tried to trade Emery, but couldn't find any takers. Emery's antics had made him unmoveable.

So the Senators moved toward the playoffs with plenty of questions. Their season was ended by the Pittsburgh Penguins; getting beaten handily in the first round of the playoffs. At the season-ending press conference, Murray announced to the media that Emery would not return to the team next season.

"He didn't, in my opinion, commit to the team in the way that we think our players have to commit," Murray said. Emery cleared waivers on June 23, 2008 and became an unrestricted free agent, leaving the

Senators on the hook for one-third of the remainder of his contract, approximately $2.25 million spread over four years.

Once believed to be the future of the franchise in net, Emery's days in the nation's capital had come to a rather abrupt end. There were no Emery-takers anywhere in the NHL; the spat between he and his now-former team had turned the rest of the league off. He was exiled to the Kontinental League.

A toned-down Emery eventually found his way back to the NHL with Philadelphia, but his fall from grace with the Senators was one of the most entertaining hockey quarrels in recent memory.

CHRIS PRONGER
EDMONTON

VS.

Chris Pronger was a hero in Edmonton – until he wanted out.

When the NHL came out of the 2004-05 lockout with a salary cap, many teams started maneuvering their rosters to position themselves properly in the new economic era. On Aug. 2, 2005 a trade that before the lockout would have been reserved for fantasy hockey leagues was made between the St. Louis Blues and Edmonton Oilers. The Blues shipped off hard-nosed defenseman Chris Pronger for Eric Brewer, Jeff Woywitka and Doug Lynch, but it was Pronger's involvement that made headlines and got Oilers fans giddy.

> ## "The hockey world turned upside down when the Oilers obtained Chris Pronger."
> ## - THN

Small-market Edmonton often had to move out its coming-of-age stars as they hit their primes because of the price tags that came with them, but with a new system in place to produce parity, Edmonton was all of a sudden in the market for acquiring one of those superstars.

"The hockey world turned upside down when the Oilers obtained Chris Pronger, the Hart Trophy and Norris Trophy winner in 2000, by sending the kind of package Edmonton had always sought under the old system to a club, St. Louis, that had previously been a buyer of big names," THN wrote back in 2005.

The Oilers had missed the playoffs the season prior to the lockout, but the addition of Pronger gave the team a stalwart to build a system around. And although the team squeaked into the playoffs as the No. 8 seed, the presence of the towering blueliner paid off with big dividends.

The Oilers knocked off the Presidents' Trophy-winning Detroit Red Wings in six games, the San Jose Sharks in six and the Anaheim Mighty Ducks in five to make a miraculous run to the Cup final. Edmonton lost to Carolina in seven games and while Cam Ward won the Conn Smythe, many argued it should have been given to Pronger, who lifted the Oilers to unexpected heights.

With 21 points in 24 playoff games, Pronger had notched the most post-season points by a defenseman since Brian Leetch put up 34 points in 1994. Pronger also became the first player to score on a penalty shot in the Cup final, achieving the feat in Game 1.

But Edmonton's new hero was about to become Public Enemy No. 1.

Four days after the final ended, Pronger requested a trade from Edmonton, where he signed a five-year contract when first acquired. Rumors of infidelity swirled around the Internet, but the truth was his wife, Lauren, wasn't happy in their new city and was the catalyst for the move. On July 3, 2006, 11 months after bringing him in, the Oilers shipped Pronger to Anaheim for Joffrey Lupul, Ladislav Smid, two first round picks and a second-rounder.

"The organization was aware of Pronger's desire to be moved early in the year, yet it rode him all the way to Game 7 of the Stanley Cup final," THN senior writer Mike Brophy wrote in 2006. "That's because even though he wished he were elsewhere, Pronger was professional when it came to doing his job. He played part of the year on a broken foot and through a portion of the playoffs with a partially separated shoulder."

But Edmontonians have a much different view on it.

Ever since the trade, Pronger has been booed whenever he's returned to Rexall Place and the nickname Public Enemy No. 1 sticks to him. The blogosphere was filled with vitriol and Oilers message boards refuse to forgive Pronger. On one hand, he was taking care of his family, on the other he was abandoning a franchise he had signed a contract with only a few days after a run to the final.

Never mind he was the leader of the magical year; the way the big guy left town left a sour taste in the mouths of Oilers fans that will linger on in the history books.

VS.

HARVARD UNIVERSITY
CORNELL UNIVERSITY

They are two of the marquee hockey schools in the Ivy League, but there's nothing elite about the way fans of Harvard and Cornell treat each other's players.

As members of the ECAC, Harvard and Cornell have been conference rivals since the 1960s. Since that time, the Crimson of Harvard have clinched 13 regular season ECAC titles and won the conference tournament eight times. Meanwhile, Cornell's Big Red have rung up nine regular season titles and 12 tourney championships. Cornell also holds two national titles to Harvard's one and owns the only undefeated season in NCAA hockey Div. I history (1969-70).

But when it comes down to it, the kids at Cornell are just a bunch of dumb farmers, while those Harvard stiffs can go jump in the ocean. Those regional stereotypes have led to a lot of mischief in the stands over the years, much of which would be frowned upon today.

Ted Donato is a former NHLer who played his college hockey at Harvard from 1987-91 and went on to coach the Crimson after he retired from the game. He remembers the very distinct way Cornell players were greeted in Harvard's rink by Crimson fans.

> **"They used to tie live chickens to the goalposts."**
> **- Ted Donato**

"They used to tie live chickens to the goalposts," Donato said. "You probably couldn't do that anymore."

In response, Cornell fans would pelt the Harvard players when they came onto the ice at the legendary Lynah Rink in Ithaca, N.Y.

"People had smuggled in fish," recalled goalie Brian Hayward, who played for Cornell from 1978-81. "And Harvard would get pelted with fish for 20 minutes."

Donato remembered fish, oranges and newspapers.

Cornell's Riley Nash could always count on rabid support when his school hosted Harvard.

"Cornell has such a great home advantage with the level of excitement and electricity in the building," he said. "It's one of the great buildings to play in."

Not that the Harvard faithful stopped with chicken wrangling.

"They would pelt me with tennis balls," Hayward said. "Anytime a 2-on-1 was developing, I would see everyone stand up in the corner of my eye, ready to pelt me if Harvard scored."

Being two of the better programs in the ECAC, the Crimson and Big Red often meet in meaningful games, so the pranks weren't the only reason to attend games.

"To get anywhere, usually those teams collide," Donato said. "You need to play with a certain level of emotion to keep pace and the kids need to enjoy it, they can't be intimidated."

And if that's too much levity for you, there's always the height of sopho-moric humor to fall back on. Donato remembered one story passed down to him from Bill Cleary, who coached the former Boston Bruin at Harvard during his freshman season. One night at Lynah, Cornell fans managed to toss a 10-foot long inflatable phallus onto the ice. The referee, quite rightly, assessed the Cornell bench a two-minute penalty to punish the Big Red for the transgressions of their fans. Cleary started screaming at the ref from Harvard's bench, prompting a visit from the very confused official.

"He skated over and said, 'What do you want me to do, I gave them a two-minute penalty,' " Donato relayed. "And Cleary said, 'Are you kid-ding? Look at the size of that thing, that's gotta be a major!' "

VS. JIM SCHOENFELD DON KOHARSKI

Thankfully the moment was caught on tape to provide evidence and even a little bit of laughter in hindsight.

The New Jersey Devils, in the playoffs for the first time since moving from Colorado a decade prior, met the Boston Bruins in the 1987-88 Prince of Wales Conference final, but it wasn't your ordinary seven-game series.

After Game 3, which the Bruins won 6-1 to take a 2-1 series lead, Devils coach Jim Schoenfeld was upset with the job done by referee Don Koharski. As Koharski left the ice and walked down the tunnel with an angry Schoenfeld in his face, Koharksi lost his balance and when he accused Schoenfeld of pushing him, it teed up one of the most unforget-table off-ice moments in NHL playoff history.

"You tripped and fell you fat pig!" Schoenfeld yelled. "Have another donut! Have another donut!"

After the incident, Schoenfeld said, "I had a point I wanted to make and he obviously didn't want to hear it. I said 'I didn't touch you. You bumped into me.' Those were the first words out of my mouth. Then he stumbled and said 'You'll never coach again' and all that kind of garbage."

The confrontation had a profound impact on the series. NHL commissioner John Ziegler suspended the Devils coach for his derogatory remarks towards the referee, but the mess didn't end without a fight. New Jersey moved to block the suspension by serving the NHL with a restraining order granted by New Jersey Superior Court judge J.F. Madden, which allowed Schoenfeld to return to the bench in Game 4.

"The New Jersey Devils cannot tolerate the injustice that has been done to Jim Schoenfeld and our organization," Devils president and GM Lou Lamoriello said in a statement at the time. "We are owed the right of a hearing and appeal."

Referee Don Koharski was the target of one of hockey's most famous tirades.

In turn, the three NHL officials who were scheduled to work Game 4, Dave Newell, Gord Broseker and Ray Scapinello, staged a wildcat strike to protest what they felt were unsafe working conditions. With fans in their seats and the teams on the ice, the game start was delayed for an hour while the league had to turn to amateur substitute officials to work the game.

When the substitutes took the ice, only one, 52-year-old Devils off-ice official Paul McInnis, wore the black and white striped referee shirt. The linesmen, 51-year-old Devils off-ice official Vin Godleski and 50-year-old Jim Sullivan, an Islanders off-ice official, started by wearing green sweat pants and yellow practice jerseys with white helmets.

> **"You tripped and fell you fat pig! Have another donut!"**
> **- Jim Schoenfeld**

The game went on and the Devils evened the series with a 3-1 win. Bruins coach Terry O'Reilly wasn't pleased with how everything played out.

"To me that wasn't a National Hockey League game," O'Reilly said at the time. "It's a shame it happened in the playoffs. It's a shame it happened at all."

The league worked out the problems with its on-ice officials and the New Jersey organization. Schoenfeld's suspension was rescinded and the league agreed to the NHL Officials' Association's demands for safer working conditions. NHL referees returned to the ice for Game 5 of the series, but more than 20 years later the incident still strikes a chord.

Both Koharski and Schoenfeld respectfully declined to be interviewed for this story and even Devils right winger Pat Verbeek – whose double-minor for roughing tipped Schoenfeld over the edge – declined.

The Bruins went on to win two of the final three games to move on to the Stanley Cup final.

VS. GORDIE HOWE
ROCKET RICHARD

Hockey's dominant performer.

An icon of the game.

A larger-than-life legend.

Apply these descriptives to Gordie Howe, or Maurice 'Rocket' Richard and they fit aptly in either case.

In some ways, Howe and Richard were kindred spirits.

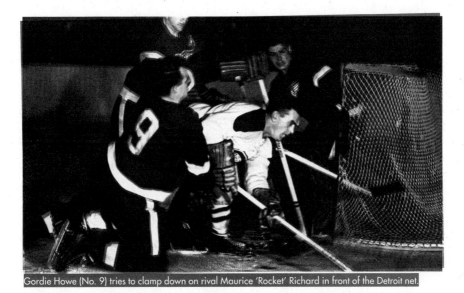

Gordie Howe (No. 9) tries to clamp down on rival Maurice 'Rocket' Richard in front of the Detroit net.

Both played right wing. Both wore No. 9. They were the spiritual leaders of their respective teams.

And yet, they were so different in their approach that they proved the perfect foil in a perfect storm.

Throughout the history of hockey, no two rivals have dominated the game and galvanized its fans in the manner that Howe and Richard did.

From 1946, the season Howe entered the NHL, through 1960, the year in which Richard bowed out of the game, this duo was as dynamic and dominant as the teams for which they skated.

Howe was the game's greatest all-around player; Richard the game's greatest goal-scorer.

Either Howe (seven times) or Richard (six) was the right winger on the NHL's First All-Star Team 13 times. On eight occasions, they filled both the First and Second Team positions. Howe led the NHL in scoring five times over that span, while Richard topped the league in goals on four occasions.

In that time frame, Richard's Montreal Canadiens won six Stanley Cups and competed in 11 Cup finals. Howe's Detroit Red Wings won the Stanley Cup four times and appeared in seven finals.

On four occasions, Howe's Wings met Richard's Habs in the final and Howe came out the winner three times. You weren't required to follow hockey closely to know of their distaste for each other. They were the most prominent faces amidst hockey's most passionate rivalry.

"I guess it was a little damn near hate," said former Detroit center Alex Delvecchio. "It was quite a rivalry. Montreal was our biggest obstacle to winning the Stanley Cup. They were a powerhouse. It made you play better, because you wanted to beat them so badly."

Both men were known as much for their toughness and dirty tactics as they were for their skill. The first time Howe and Richard met on the ice, the veteran Richard, 25, challenged the rookie Howe, 18, to a fight.

Howe knocked out Richard with one punch.

Howe's legendary elbows decked many unsuspecting opponents. "You had to cope with the stick, the elbows, and then that body," Hall of Fame Montreal player and coach Toe Blake explained to Tim Burke of the Montreal *Gazette* in a 1979 interview.

> ## "The Rocket had a temper and it backfired on him at times."
> ## - Budd Lynch

Richard was more open with his miscreant deeds and wasn't afraid to snap his stick over the back of an opponent that was getting on his nerves. "The Rocket disdained finesse," former Canadiens managing director Frank Selke wrote in a *Canadian* magazine piece.

In his 1999 book, *Gordie Howe: My Hockey Memories*, Howe wrote: "I don't think I played with anyone as driven and determined as Richard... In terms of raw talent and competitiveness, he was among the best ever and his speed and nose for the net haven't been matched before or since."

It was their style as much as anything that separated fans into two camps when it came to Howe and Richard. "You can still start a fist fight in certain drinking establishments in the old six cities by simply stating that Richard was vastly superior to Howe, or vice versa," authors Chrys Goyens and Alan Turowetz surmised in their 1986 Canadiens history book *Lions In Winter*.

Known as 'Mr. Hockey,' Howe was the company man, the type of boy a girl's mother hoped her daughter would bring home to meet the family. Many believed that had Howe, with his stature in the game, stepped forward into a greater role, teammate Ted Lindsay's bid to launch the NHLPA in 1957 would have met with success.

Other historians cite the Richard Riot, when fans disrupted a March 17, 1955 Detroit-Montreal game at the Forum to protest NHL president Clarence Campbell's season-ending suspension of Richard following a vicious stick-swinging battle in a game at Boston, as the launching pad for the Quebec separatist movement, viewing Richard more so as a cultural icon than merely a hockey player.

There's no doubt that Richard was a rebel, as fiery as his nickname indicated. He penned a column for a French-language newspaper during his playing days and frequently challenged Campbell's handling of the league with his writings.

"The Rocket had a temper and it backfired on him at times," Red Wings Hall of Fame broadcaster Budd Lynch said. "That was the one thing that gave Gordie the edge."

Howe and Richard are frequently paralleled to Lou Gehrig and Babe Ruth, the New York Yankees stars who dominated baseball in the 1930s. Iron man Gehrig was the perennially consistent producer with machine-like precision; Ruth the record-breaking explosive power hitter who set his own rules and whose aura appeared larger than the game itself.

In 1953, Canadian Press commissioned a poll of NHL writers. In it, Howe was proclaimed the league's best player and Richard the NHL's most colorful performer.

"There's no doubt that Gordie was better than Maurice," acknowledged Richard's younger brother Henri in a 1980 interview with the Gazette's Burke. "But build two rinks across from one another. Then put Gordie in one and Maurice in the other and see which one would be filled."

Hall of Famer King Clancy was prepared with the answer. "The rink that the Rocket was playing in would be jammed and the overflow from it would be going into the other rink to watch Howe," Clancy said.

Richard set the bar – in 1944-45, he was the league's first 50-goal scorer and the first with 500 career NHL goals, ending up as the NHL's all-time goal and point-scoring leader.

"The man made the league what it is today so the rest of us could make a living at it." said Howe, who came along and surpassed the Rocket's totals.

Their rivalry knew no bounds and it wasn't restricted to their playing days.

In 1997, Howe announced plans to make a comeback at the age of 69, playing one shift for the International League's Detroit Vipers.

Richard, who was still penning a column for *La Presse* at the time, took Howe to task. "It's completely ridiculous," Richard wrote. "A publicity stunt."

Discussing Richard's comments during a conference call to promote his return to the ice, Howe was equally terse. "It took me 40 years to get to like the guy," Howe said. "He ruined it in one sentence."

VS. LARRY BROOKS JOHN TORTORELLA

Since he first became an NHL head coach in 2001, John Tortorella never has been known to soft-pedal or shield his passionate opinions from the hockey-watching public and media.

So when the volatile, Stanley-Cup-winning bench boss became coach of the New York Rangers halfway through the 2008-09 season, it was only natural that Tortorella eventually would disagree with professional hockey columnists paid to present strong opinions.

And given that Larry Brooks – New York *Post* columnist and longtime Rangers correspondent for *The Hockey News* – is acknowledged as one of the strongest voices in the sport today, it was only proper that he and Tortorella would quickly and publicly clash on numerous occasions.

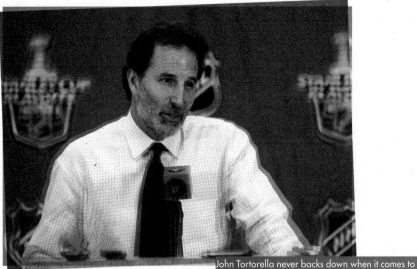

John Tortorella never backs down when it comes to media scrums.

The first time Brooks and Tortorella sparred actually came in late April of 2007, when Tortorella was coaching the Tampa Bay Lightning.

After the Bolts had been shut out 3-0 by New Jersey in Game 5 of their first round playoff series, Brooks asked Tortorella questions in a post-game media scrum; Tortorella had been vague or combative in his answers – and tempers soon raised, with the Lightning coach first telling Brooks to, "get the f--- out of here," and Brooks replying, "f--- off."

Their next memorable public spat took place in January of 2010, by which time Tortorella had been Rangers coach for nearly a year. Brooks had asked a question pertaining to why Blueshirts star Marian Gaborik fought Flyers pest Daniel Carcillo; but Tortorella – still displeased by a previous Brooks column ripping defenseman Wade Redden – refused to answer:

Tortorella: I'm not going to answer any questions from you.
Brooks: You're not? Oh good, I'll speculate then.

Later in the same media scrum, Tortorella posed a question for Brooks:

Tortorella: Have you ever fought before?
Brooks: Yeah.
Tortorella: You have?
Brooks: Yeah. Why, are you challenging me?

Tortorella: No, no I'm not challenging you….you were probably beat up at the bus stop most of the time.
Brooks: You're a great representative of the city, you know that?

To his credit, Brooks didn't want to make his feud with Tortorella the focus of post-game Rangers press conferences. And he refused to shy away from his consistent criticisms of Tortorella (whom he called a "dictator" in an earlier column), Rangers management and the team's inability to make the playoffs in Tortorella's first two seasons.

In a *Post* column published the day after the Rangers failed to make the 2010 playoffs, Brooks summarized the situation:

John Tortorella's last two full seasons behind an NHL bench have resulted in finishes of 30th overall with the Lightning in 2007-08 and 21st overall (in 2009-10). He has a small-market mentality, does not understand at all what New York is about and is a professional bully who has earned the enmity of nearly everyone with whom he has come into contact.

I regret that I have become so personally entwined with this coach that I'm compelled to stipulate that I am not engaged in a vendetta against him. I have neither written about nor spoken of the breakdown in our relationship and have no interest in doing so.

But I must state that my relentless criticism of Tortorella – whom, by the way, I enthusiastically endorsed for the job a week before he replaced Tom Renney – is the cause of the rift and not its effect.

I do not believe a coach can win in this league by creating an environment of underlying tension, or by constantly screaming at players, or by changing line combinations every five minutes, or by obsessing over players staying out of the penalty box at the expense of protecting teammates, or by trying to win with two forward lines.

A veteran NHL executive who has experience dealing with both Brooks and Tortorella over the past decade said that, while their distaste for one another may make for gripping drama, it does neither party much good.

"If you talk to both guys 1-on-1, it's hard not to like them," said the executive, who spoke under condition of anonymity ("It would be a race to see who would want me dead first," he laughed). "But together, they're like sugar in a gas tank."

"With Larry, you know it's part of his job to be critical — even though I must say, having been roasted by the media, it's not easy to read harsh criticisms about yourself or your organization," the executive continued.

"Together, they're like sugar in a gas tank."
- NHL exec

"I'm sure even Larry would tell you his job in New York is much harder to do on a day-to-day basis now, because people think, whether they're right or not, he has an ax to grind. But he's been part of that community for a long time, which makes me wonder why John wants to continue butting heads with him.

"And with John, I know people have tried to tell him many times that you can't really ever win a fight with a media member. But that never stops him from doing what he thinks is right, even when he comes off looking like the bad guy."

Photo credits

Acknowledgements

This book was put together by a scrappy and determined staff that fought long odds and came out with a winner, much like many of the characters they wrote about in the following pages.

THN editor-in-chief Jason Kay initiated the project, while editor Ryan Kennedy pulled all the material together.

A big thanks to all the THN staffers, interns and correspondents who made this book a reality.

THN staff: Jason Kay, Brian Costello, Edward Fraser, Ryan Kennedy, Ryan Dixon, John Grigg, Ken Campbell, Adam Proteau, Rory Boylen, Jamie Hodgson, Erika Vanderveer and Ted Cooper.

THN correspondents and freelancers: Denis Gibbons, Mike Loftus, Luke Decock, Rob Tychkowski, Adrian Dater, Phil Janack, Tim Campbell, Bob Duff, Murray Pam, Joe Starkey, Mike Zeisberger, Neil Hodge, Mike Heika, Risto Pakarinen, Michael Traikos and Wayne Fish.

Interns: Hilary Hagerman, Nikki Cook, Nick Spector, Ronnie Shuker, Kevin Hall, Cory Johnson, Dustin Pollack, Kyle Palantzas, Brandon Macdonald, Ryan Williams and Matthew Krebs.

The brass: THN publisher Caroline Andrews and Transcontinental book publisher Jean Pare.